PHP AND WBEMSCRIPTING

Working with ExecQuery

Richard Thomas Edwards

CONTENTS

PHP is not Perlscript

It is even cooler

WHEN I FIRST STARTED WORKING WITH PHP, MY FIRST THOUGHT WAS PHP LOOKS JUST LIKE Perlscript. I was wrong, it is even cooler!.

Furthermore, I didn't need to install IIS or work through ISS or HTML to work with and test my scripts. I downloaded the php-5.2.10-nts-Win32-VC6-x86 MSI Installer, went with the defaults and popped my "test.php" with the usual "Hello world" up on my desktop. I then ran the PHP.exe from the php folder, then right clicked on the test.php and made the run with association from there.

The end result:

Below is the script I used to create the first file:

```
<?php

function GetValue($prop, $obj)
```

```
{
    $n = $prop->Name . " = ";
    $tempstr = $obj->GetObjectText_(0);
    $pos = strpos($tempstr, $n);
    if($pos != FALSE)
    {
        $pos = $pos + strlen($n);
        $tempstr = substr($tempstr, $pos, strlen($tempstr));
        $pos = strpos($tempstr, ";");
        $tempstr = substr($tempstr, 0, $pos);
        $tempstr = str_replace("{" , "", $tempstr);
        $tempstr = str_replace("{" , "", $tempstr);
        $tempstr = str_replace('"' , "", $tempstr);
        if($prop->CIMType == 101)
        {
            if(strlen($tempstr) > 13)
            {
                $tempstr = substr($tempstr, 4,2) . "/" . substr($tempstr, 6, 2) . "/" .
substr($tempstr, 0, 4) . " " . substr($tempstr, 8, 2) . ":" . substr($tempstr, 10, 2) .
":" . substr($tempstr, 12, 2);
                return($tempstr);

            }
        }
        else
        {
            return($tempstr);
        }
    }
    else
    {
        return "";
    }
```

```
}
$l = new COM ("Wbemscripting.SWbemLocator");
$svc = $l->ConnectServer(".", "root\\cimv2");
$svc->Security_->AuthenticationLevel = 6;
$svc->Security_->ImpersonationLevel = 3;
$objs = $svc->ExecQuery("Select * From Win32_Process");

$ws = new COM ("WScript.Shell");
$fso = new COM ("Scripting.FileSystemObject");
$txtstream        =        $fso->OpenTextFile($ws->CurrentDirectory     .
"\\Win32_Process.html", 2, TRUE, -2);
$txtstream->WriteLine("<html>");
$txtstream->WriteLine("<head>");
$txtstream->WriteLine("<style type='text/css'>");
$txtstream->WriteLine("th");
$txtstream->WriteLine("{");
$txtstream->WriteLine("COLOR: darkred;");
$txtstream->WriteLine("BACKGROUND-COLOR: white;");
$txtstream->WriteLine("FONT-FAMILY: Cambria, serif;");
$txtstream->WriteLine("FONT-SIZE: 12px;");
$txtstream->WriteLine("text-align: left;");
$txtstream->WriteLine("white-Space: nowrap;");
$txtstream->WriteLine("}");
$txtstream->WriteLine("td");
$txtstream->WriteLine("{");
$txtstream->WriteLine("COLOR: navy;");
$txtstream->WriteLine("BACKGROUND-COLOR: white;");
$txtstream->WriteLine("FONT-FAMILY: font-family: Cambria, serif;");
$txtstream->WriteLine("FONT-SIZE: 12px;");
$txtstream->WriteLine("text-align: left;");
$txtstream->WriteLine("white-Space: nowrap;");
$txtstream->WriteLine("}");
$txtstream->WriteLine("</style>");
```

```php
$txtstream->WriteLine("<title>Win32_Process</title>");
$txtstream->WriteLine("</head>");
$txtstream->WriteLine("<body>");
$txtstream->WriteLine("<table Border='2' cellpadding='3' cellspacing='3'>");
$txtstream->WriteLine("<tr>");
foreach($objs as $obj)
{
    foreach($obj->Properties_ as $prop)
    {
      $txtstream->WriteLine("<th align='left' nowrap='true'>" . $prop->Name .
"</th>");
    }
}
$txtstream->WriteLine("</tr>");
foreach($objs as $obj)
{
    $txtstream->WriteLine("<tr>");
    foreach($obj->Properties_ as $prop)
    {
      $txtstream->WriteLine("<td        align='left'     nowrap='true'>"     .
GetValue($prop, $obj) . "</td>");
    }
    $txtstream->WriteLine("</tr>");
}
$txtstream->WriteLine("</table>");
$txtstream->WriteLine("</body>");
$txtstream->WriteLine("</html>");
$txtstream->close();

?>
```

The proof that it worked:

Caption	CommandLine
System Idle Process	
System	
smss.exe	
csrss.exe	
wininit.exe	wininit.exe
csrss.exe	
services.exe	
lsass.exe	C:\Windows\system32\lsass.exe
winlogon.exe	winlogon.exe
svchost.exe	C:\Windows\system32\svchost.exe -k DcomLaunch
svchost.exe	C:\Windows\system32\svchost.exe -k RPCSS
dwm.exe	dwm.exe\
NVDisplay.Container.exe	\C:\Program Files\NVIDIA Corporation\Display.NvContainer\NVDisplay.Container.exe\ -s NVDispla
svchost.exe	C:\Windows\System32\svchost.exe -k LocalServiceNetworkRestricted
svchost.exe	C:\Windows\system32\svchost.exe -k netsvcs
svchost.exe	C:\Windows\system32\svchost.exe -k LocalService
svchost.exe	C:\Windows\system32\svchost.exe -k NetworkService
svchost.exe	C:\Windows\System32\svchost.exe -k LocalSystemNetworkRestricted
svchost.exe	C:\Windows\system32\svchost.exe -k LocalServiceNoNetwork
spoolsv.exe	C:\Windows\System32\spoolsv.exe
svchost.exe	C:\Windows\system32\svchost.exe -k apphost
OfficeClickToRun.exe	\C:\Program Files\Common Files\Microsoft Shared\ClickToRun\OfficeClickToRun.exe\ /service
svchost.exe	C:\Windows\system32\svchost.exe -k ftpsvc
ibguard.exe	\C:\Program Files (x86)\Embarcadero\InterBase2017_gds_db\Interbase2017\bin\ibguard.exe\ -i \C:\
inetinfo.exe	C:\Windows\system32\inetsrv\inetinfo.exe
KindleDesktopService.exe	\C:\Program Files (x86)\Amazon\KindleAddIn\Service\KindleDesktopService.exe\
NVDisplay.Container.exe	\C:\Program Files\NVIDIA Corporation\Display.NvContainer\NVDisplay.Container.exe\ -f \C:\Progi
MsDtsSrvr.exe	\C:\Program Files\Microsoft SQL Server\110\DTS\Binn\MsDtsSrvr.exe\

So, you can teach old dogs new tricks!

We're going to be using the code template above. Because we are going to be doing both horizontal and vertical views and because we're going to be doing event driven code, I thought it wise to use the dictionary objects to help make all the examples work regardless of whether or not we're running event driven code.

Here's a look at the revised code:

```php
<?php

$v = 0;
$x = 0;
$y = 0;

$nd = new COM("Scripting.Dictionary");
$rd = new COM("Scripting.Dictionary");

function GetValue($prop, $obj)
{
    $n = $prop->Name . " = ";
    $tempstr = $obj->GetObjectText_(0);
    $pos = strpos($tempstr, $n);
    if($pos != FALSE)
    {
        $pos = $pos + strlen($n);
        $tempstr = substr($tempstr, $pos, strlen($tempstr));
        $pos = strpos($tempstr, ";");
        $tempstr = substr($tempstr, 0, $pos);
        $tempstr = str_replace("{" , "", $tempstr);
        $tempstr = str_replace("{" , "", $tempstr);
        $tempstr = str_replace('"' , "", $tempstr);
        if($prop->CIMType == 101)
        {
            if(strlen($tempstr) > 13)
            {
                $tempstr = substr($tempstr, 4,2) . "/" . substr($tempstr, 6, 2) . "/" . substr($tempstr, 0, 4) . " " . substr($tempstr, 8, 2) . ":" . substr($tempstr, 10, 2) . ":" . substr($tempstr, 12, 2);
```

```
          return($tempstr);


        }
      }
      else
      {
        return($tempstr);
      }
    }
    else
    {
      return "";
    }
}


$l = new COM ("Wbemscripting.SWbemLocator");
$svc = $l->ConnectServer(".", "root\\cimv2");
$svc->Security_->AuthenticationLevel = 6;
$svc->Security_->ImpersonationLevel = 3;
$objs = $svc->ExecQuery("Select * From Win32_Process");
$obj = $objs->ItemIndex(0);
foreach($obj->Properties_ as $prop)
{
  $nd->Add($x, $prop->Name);
  $x=$x+1;
}
$x=0;

foreach($objs as $obj)
{
    $cd = new COM("Scripting.Dictionary");
    foreach($obj->Properties_ as $prop)
    {
```

```
        $value = GetValue($prop, $obj);
        $cd->Add($x, $value);
        $x = $x+1;
      }
      $rd->Add($y, $cd);
      $x=0;
      $y=$y+1;
    }


    $ws = new COM ("WScript.Shell");
    $fso = new COM ("Scripting.FileSystemObject");
    $txtstream        =        $fso->OpenTextFile($ws->CurrentDirectory      .
"\\Win32_Process.html", 2, TRUE, -2);
    $txtstream->WriteLine("<html>");
    $txtstream->WriteLine("<head>");
    $txtstream->WriteLine("<style type='text/css'>");
    $txtstream->WriteLine("th");
    $txtstream->WriteLine("{");
    $txtstream->WriteLine("COLOR: darkred;");
    $txtstream->WriteLine("BACKGROUND-COLOR: white;");
    $txtstream->WriteLine("FONT-FAMILY: Cambria, serif;");
    $txtstream->WriteLine("FONT-SIZE: 12px;");
    $txtstream->WriteLine("text-align: left;");
    $txtstream->WriteLine("white-Space: nowrap;");
    $txtstream->WriteLine("}");
    $txtstream->WriteLine("td");
    $txtstream->WriteLine("{");
    $txtstream->WriteLine("COLOR: navy;");
    $txtstream->WriteLine("BACKGROUND-COLOR: white;");
    $txtstream->WriteLine("FONT-FAMILY: font-family: Cambria, serif;");
    $txtstream->WriteLine("FONT-SIZE: 12px;");
    $txtstream->WriteLine("text-align: left;");
    $txtstream->WriteLine("white-Space: nowrap;");
```

```
$txtstream->WriteLine("}");
$txtstream->WriteLine("</style>");
$txtstream->WriteLine("<title>Win32_Process</title>");
$txtstream->WriteLine("</head>");
$txtstream->WriteLine("<body>");
$txtstream->WriteLine("<table Border='2' cellpadding='3' cellspacing='3'>");
$txtstream->WriteLine("<tr>");
for($a=0; $a < sizeof($nd->keys);$a ++)
{
    $txtstream->WriteLine("<th    align='left'   nowrap='true'>"   .    $nd-
>items[$a] . "</th>");
}
$txtstream->WriteLine("</tr>");
for($y=0; $y < sizeof($rd->keys);$y ++)
{
    $txtstream->WriteLine("<tr>");
    $cd = $rd->items[$y];
    for($a=0; $a < sizeof($cd->keys);$a ++)
    {
        $txtstream->WriteLine("<td    align='left'   nowrap='true'>"   .   $cd-
>items[$a] . "</td>");
    }
    $txtstream->WriteLine("</tr>");
}

$txtstream->WriteLine("</table>");
$txtstream->WriteLine("</body>");
$txtstream->WriteLine("</html>");
$txtstream->close();

?>
```

And the proof that while a bit slower than the original:

Caption	CommandLine
System Idle Process	
System	
smss.exe	
csrss.exe	
wininit.exe	wininit.exe
csrss.exe	
services.exe	
lsass.exe	C:\Windows\system32\lsass.exe
winlogon.exe	winlogon.exe
svchost.exe	C:\Windows\system32\svchost.exe -k DcomLaunch
svchost.exe	C:\Windows\system32\svchost.exe -k RPCSS
dwm.exe	\dwm.exe\
NVDisplay.Container.exe	C:\Program Files\NVIDIA Corporation\Display.NvContainer\NVDisplay.Container.exe\ -s NVDispla
svchost.exe	C:\Windows\System32\svchost.exe -k LocalServiceNetworkRestricted
svchost.exe	C:\Windows\system32\svchost.exe -k netsvcs
svchost.exe	C:\Windows\system32\svchost.exe -k LocalService
svchost.exe	C:\Windows\system32\svchost.exe -k NetworkService
svchost.exe	C:\Windows\System32\svchost.exe -k LocalSystemNetworkRestricted
svchost.exe	C:\Windows\system32\svchost.exe -k LocalServiceNoNetwork
spoolsv.exe	C:\Windows\System32\spoolsv.exe
svchost.exe	C:\Windows\system32\svchost.exe -k apphost
OfficeClickToRun.exe	C:\Program Files\Common Files\Microsoft Shared\ClickToRun\OfficeClickToRun.exe\ \service
svchost.exe	C:\Windows\system32\svchost.exe -k ftpsvc
ibguard.exe	C:\Program Files (x86)\Embarcadero\InterBase2017_gds_db\Interbase2017\bin\ibguard.exe\ -i \C:
inetinfo.exe	C:\Windows\system32\inetsrv\inetinfo.exe
KindleDesktopService.exe	C:\Program Files (x86)\Amazon\KindleAddIn\Service\KindleDesktopService.exe\
NVDisplay.Container.exe	C:\Program Files\NVIDIA Corporation\Display.NvContainer\NVDisplay.Container.exe\ -f \C:\Prog
MsDtsSrvr.exe	C:\Program Files\Microsoft SQL Server\110\DTS\Binn\MsDtsSrvr.exe\

Okay, so let's get started on the routines.

ASP Reports

All of the code here is cut and paste. You can copy the code inside the function or copy the code, include the function and then call it one the routine is finished.

I've also included some stylesheets at the end of this book for you to add to each of the programs. Enjoy!

Begin Code

```
function Write_The_Code()
{
    $ws = new COM("WScript.Shell");
    $fso = new COM("Scripting.FileSystemObject");
    $txtstream        =        $fso->OpenTextFile($ws->CurrentDirectory      .
"\\Win32_Process.html", 2, true, -2);
    $txtstream->WriteLine("<html xmlns=\"http://www.w3.org/1999/xhtml\">");
    $txtstream->WriteLine("<head>");
    $txtstream->WriteLine("<title>Win32_Process</title>");
    $txtstream->WriteLine("</head>");
    $txtstream->WriteLine("<body>");
    $txtstream->WriteLine("<%");
    $txtstream->WriteLine("Response.Write(\"<table cellpadding=2 cellspacing=2>\"
& vbcrlf)");
    $txtstream->WriteLine("Response.Write(\"<tr>\" & vbcrlf)");
    for($a=0; $a < sizeof($nd->keys);$a ++)
    {
        $txtstream->WriteLine("Response.Write(\"<th style='color:darkred;font-
size:10px;font-family:Cambria, serif;' align='left' nowrap>" . $nd->items[$a].
"</th>\" & vbcrlf)");
    }
    $txtstream->WriteLine("Response.Write(\"</tr>\" & vbcrlf)");
```

Horizontal No Additional Tags

```
for($y=0; $y < sizeof($rd->keys);$y ++)
{
    $txtstream->WriteLine("Response.Write(\"<tr>\" & vbcrlf)");
    $cd = $rd->items[$y];
    for($a=0; $a < sizeof($nd->keys);$a ++)
    {
        $txtstream->WriteLine("Response.Write(\"<td style='color:navy;font-size:10px;font-family:Cambria, serif;' align='left' nowrap>" . $cd->items[$a] . "</td>\" & vbcrlf)");
    }
    $txtstream->WriteLine("Response.Write(\"</tr>\" & vbcrlf)");
}
```

Horizontal Using A Button

```
for($y=0; $y < sizeof($rd->keys);$y ++)
{
    $txtstream->WriteLine("Response.Write(\"<tr>\" & vbcrlf)");
    $cd = $rd->items[$y];
    for($a=0; $a < sizeof($nd->keys);$a ++)
    {
        $txtstream->WriteLine("Response.Write(\"<td style='color:navy;font-size:10px;font-family:Cambria, serif;' align='left' nowrap><input Type= button value=\"\" . $cd->items[$a] . \"\"></input></td>\" & vbcrlf)");
    }
    $txtstream->WriteLine("Response.Write(\"</tr>\" & vbcrlf)");
}
```

Horizontal Using A ComboBox

```
for($y=0; $y < sizeof($rd->keys);$y ++)
```

```
{
    $txtstream->WriteLine("Response.Write(\"<tr>\" & vbcrlf)");
    $cd = $rd->items[$y];
    for($a=0; $a < sizeof($nd->keys);$a ++)
    {
        $txtstream->WriteLine("Response.Write(\"<td style='font-family:Calibri,
Sans-Serif;font-size: 12px;color:navy;' align='left' nowrap='true'><select><option
value = '"  . $cd->items[$a] . "'>"  . $cd->items[$a] . "</option></select></td>\"  .
vbcrlf)");
    }
    $txtstream->WriteLine("Response.Write(\"</tr>\" & vbcrlf)");
}
```

Horizontal Using A Div

```
for($y=0; $y < sizeof($rd->keys);$y ++)
{
    $txtstream->WriteLine("Response.Write(\"<tr>\" & vbcrlf)");
    $cd = $rd->items[$y];
    for($a=0; $a < sizeof($nd->keys);$a ++)
    {

        $txtstream->WriteLine("Response.Write(\"<td style='color:navy;font-
size:10px;font-family:Cambria, serif;' align='left' nowrap><div>"  . $cd->items[$a]
. "</div></td>\" & vbcrlf)");

    }
    $txtstream->WriteLine("Response.Write(\"</tr>\" & vbcrlf)");
}
```

Horizontal Using A Link

```
for($y=0; $y < sizeof($rd->keys);$y ++)
{
    $txtstream->WriteLine("Response.Write(\"<tr>\" & vbcrlf)");
```

```
    $cd = $rd->items[$y];
    for($a=0; $a < sizeof($nd->keys);$a ++)
    {
  $txtstream->WriteLine("Response.Write(\"<td style='font-family:Calibri, Sans-
Serif;font-size: 12px;color:navy;' align='left' nowrap='true'><a href='" . $cd-
>items[$a] . "'>" . $cd->items[$a] . "</a></td>\" . vbcrlf)");
    }
    $txtstream->WriteLine("Response.Write(\"</tr>\" & vbcrlf)");
  }
```

Horizontal Using A ListBox

```
  for($y=0; $y < sizeof($rd->keys);$y ++)
  {
    $txtstream->WriteLine("Response.Write(\"<tr>\" & vbcrlf)");
    $cd = $rd->items[$y];
    for($a=0; $a < sizeof($nd->keys);$a ++)
    {
      $txtstream->WriteLine("Response.Write(\"<td style='font-family:Calibri,
Sans-Serif;font-size: 12px;color:navy;' align='left' nowrap='true'><select
multiple><option value = '" . $cd->items[$a] . "'>" . $cd->items[$a] .
"</option></select></td>\" . vbcrlf)");
    }
    $txtstream->WriteLine("Response.Write(\"</tr>\" & vbcrlf)");
  }
```

Horizontal Using A Span

```
  for($y=0; $y < sizeof($rd->keys);$y ++)
  {
    $txtstream->WriteLine("Response.Write(\"<tr>\" & vbcrlf)");
    $cd = $rd->items[$y];
    for($a=0; $a < sizeof($nd->keys);$a ++)
    {
      $txtstream->WriteLine("Response.Write(\"<td style='color:navy;font-
size:10px;font-family:Cambria, serif;' align='left' nowrap><span>" . $cd-
>items[$a] . "</span></td>\" & vbcrlf)");
```

```
      }
      $txtstream->WriteLine("Response.Write(\"</tr>\" & vbcrlf)");
   }
```

Horizontal Using A Textarea

```
   for($y=0; $y < sizeof($rd->keys);$y ++)
   {
      $txtstream->WriteLine("Response.Write(\"<tr>\" & vbcrlf)");
      $cd = $rd->items[$y];
      for($a=0; $a < sizeof($nd->keys);$a ++)
      {
          $txtstream->WriteLine("Response.Write(\"<td style='color:navy;font-
size:10px;font-family:Cambria, serif;' align='left' nowrap><textarea>" . $cd-
>items[$a] . "</textarea></td>\" & vbcrlf)");
      }
      $txtstream->WriteLine("Response.Write(\"</tr>\" & vbcrlf)");
   }
```

Horizontal Using A TextBox

```
   for($y=0; $y < sizeof($rd->keys);$y ++)
   {
      $txtstream->WriteLine("Response.Write(\"<tr>\" & vbcrlf)");
      $cd = $rd->items[$y];
      for($a=0; $a < sizeof($nd->keys);$a ++)
      {
          $txtstream->WriteLine("Response.Write(\"<td style='color:navy;font-
size:10px;font-family:Cambria, serif;' align='left' nowrap><input Type=text
value=\"\" . $cd->items[$a] . \"\"></input></td>\" & vbcrlf)");

      }
      $txtstream->WriteLine("Response.Write(\"</tr>\" & vbcrlf)");
   }
```

Vertical No Additional Controls

```
for($a=0; $a < sizeof($nd->keys);$a ++)
{
    $txtstream->WriteLine("Response.Write(\"<tr><th style='color:darkred;font-
size:10px;font-family:Cambria, serif;' align='left' nowrap>" . $nd->items[$a].
"</th>\" & vbcrlf)");
    for($y=0; $y < sizeof($rd->keys);$y ++)
    {
        $cd = $rd->items[$y];
    $txtstream->WriteLine("Response.Write(\"<td style='color:navy;font-
size:10px;font-family:Cambria, serif;' align='left' nowrap>" . $cd->items[$a] .
"</td>\" & vbcrlf)");
    }
    $txtstream->WriteLine("Response.Write(\"</tr>\" & vbcrlf)");
}
```

Vertical Using A Button

```
for($a=0; $a < sizeof($nd->keys);$a ++)
{
    $txtstream->WriteLine("Response.Write(\"<tr><th style='color:darkred;font-
size:10px;font-family:Cambria, serif;' align='left' nowrap>" . $nd->items[$a].
"</th>\" & vbcrlf)");
for($y=0; $y < sizeof($rd->keys);$y ++)
{
    $cd = $rd->items[$y];
    $txtstream->WriteLine("Response.Write(\"<td style='color:navy;font-
size:10px;font-family:Cambria, serif;' align='left' nowrap><input Type= button
value=\"\" . $cd->items[$a] . \"\"></input></td>\" & vbcrlf)");
}
    $txtstream->WriteLine("Response.Write(\"</tr>\" & vbcrlf)");
}
```

Vertical Using A ComboBox

```
for($a=0; $a < sizeof($nd->keys);$a ++)
{
    $txtstream->WriteLine("Response.Write(\"<tr><th style='color:darkred;font-
size:10px;font-family:Cambria, serif;' align='left' nowrap>" . $nd->items[$a].
"</th>\" & vbcrlf)");
    for($y=0; $y < sizeof($rd->keys);$y ++)
    {
        $cd = $rd->items[$y];
    $txtstream->WriteLine("Response.Write(\"<td style='font-family:Calibri, Sans-
Serif;font-size: 12px;color:navy;' align='left' nowrap='true'><select><option value =
'" . $cd->items[$a] . "'>" . $cd->items[$a] . "</option></select></td>\" .
vbcrlf)");
    }
    $txtstream->WriteLine("Response.Write(\"</tr>\" & vbcrlf)");
}
```

Vertical Using A Div

```
for($a=0; $a < sizeof($nd->keys);$a ++)
{
    $txtstream->WriteLine("Response.Write(\"<tr><th style='color:darkred;font-
size:10px;font-family:Cambria, serif;' align='left' nowrap>" . $nd->items[$a].
"</th>\" & vbcrlf)");
    for($y=0; $y < sizeof($rd->keys);$y ++)
    {
        $cd = $rd->items[$y];
    $txtstream->WriteLine("Response.Write(\"<td style='color:navy;font-
size:10px;font-family:Cambria, serif;' align='left' nowrap><div>" . $cd->items[$a]
. "</div></td>\" & vbcrlf)");
    }
    $txtstream->WriteLine("Response.Write(\"</tr>\" & vbcrlf)")
}
```

Vertical Using A Link

```
  for($a=0; $a < sizeof($nd->keys);$a ++)
  {
    $txtstream->WriteLine("Response.Write(\"<tr><th style='color:darkred;font-
size:10px;font-family:Cambria, serif;' align='left' nowrap>" . $nd->items[$a].
"</th>\" & vbcrlf)");
    for($y=0; $y < sizeof($rd->keys);$y ++)
    {
      $cd = $rd->items[$y];
  $txtstream->WriteLine("Response.Write(\"<td style='font-family:Calibri, Sans-
Serif;font-size: 12px;color:navy;' align='left' nowrap='true'><a href='" . $cd-
>items[$a] . "'>" . $cd->items[$a] . "</a></td>\" . vbcrlf)");
    }
    $txtstream->WriteLine("Response.Write(\"</tr>\" & vbcrlf)");
  }
```

Vertical Using A ListBox

```
  for($a=0; $a < sizeof($nd->keys);$a ++)
  {
    $txtstream->WriteLine("Response.Write(\"<tr><th style='color:darkred;font-
size:10px;font-family:Cambria, serif;' align='left' nowrap>" . $nd->items[$a].
"</th>\" & vbcrlf)");
    for($y=0; $y < sizeof($rd->keys);$y ++)
    {
      $cd = $rd->items[$y];
      $txtstream->WriteLine("Response.Write(\"<td style='font-family:Calibri,
Sans-Serif;font-size: 12px;color:navy;' align='left' nowrap='true'><select
multiple><option value = '" . $cd->items[$a] . "'>" . $cd->items[$a] .
"</option></select></td>\" . vbcrlf)");
    }
    $txtstream->WriteLine("Response.Write(\"</tr>\" & vbcrlf)");
  }
```

Vertical Using A Span

```
for($a=0; $a < sizeof($nd->keys);$a ++)
{
    $txtstream->WriteLine("Response.Write(\"<tr><th style='color:darkred;font-
size:10px;font-family:Cambria, serif;' align='left' nowrap>" . $nd->items[$a].
"</th>\" & vbcrlf)");
    for($y=0; $y < sizeof($rd->keys);$y ++)
    {
        $cd = $rd->items[$y];
$txtstream->WriteLine("Response.Write(\"<td style='color:navy;font-
size:10px;font-family:Cambria, serif;' align='left' nowrap><span>" . $cd-
>items[$a] . "</span></td>\" & vbcrlf)");
    }
    $txtstream->WriteLine("Response.Write(\"</tr>\" & vbcrlf)");
}
```

Vertical Using A Textarea

```
for($a=0; $a < sizeof($nd->keys);$a ++)
{
    $txtstream->WriteLine("Response.Write(\"<tr><th style='color:darkred;font-
size:10px;font-family:Cambria, serif;' align='left' nowrap>" . $nd->items[$a].
"</th>\" & vbcrlf)");
    for($y=0; $y < sizeof($rd->keys);$y ++)
    {
        $cd = $rd->items[$y];
$txtstream->WriteLine("Response.Write(\"<td style='color:navy;font-
size:10px;font-family:Cambria, serif;' align='left' nowrap><textarea>" . $cd-
>items[$a] . "</textarea></td>\" & vbcrlf)");
    }
    $txtstream->WriteLine("Response.Write(\"</tr>\" & vbcrlf)");
}
```

Vertical Using A TextBox

```
for($a=0; $a < sizeof($nd->keys);$a ++)
```

```
    {
        $txtstream->WriteLine("Response.Write(\"<tr><th style='color:darkred;font-
size:10px;font-family:Cambria, serif;' align='left' nowrap>"  . $nd->items[$a].
"</th>\" & vbcrlf)");
        for($y=0; $y < sizeof($rd->keys);$y ++)
        {
            $cd = $rd->items[$y];
    $txtstream->WriteLine("Response.Write(\"<td style='color:navy;font-
size:10px;font-family:Cambria, serif;' align='left' nowrap><input Type=text
value=\"\"  . $cd->items[$a] . \"\"></input></td>\" & vbcrlf)");
        }
        $txtstream->WriteLine("Response.Write(\"</tr>\" & vbcrlf)");
    }
```

End Code

```
    $txtstream->WriteLine("Response.Write(\"</table>\" & vbcrlf)");
    $txtstream->WriteLine("%>");
    $txtstream->WriteLine("</body>");
    $txtstream->WriteLine("</html>");
    $txtstream->Close();

}
```

ASP Tables

Begin Code

function Write_The_Code()

```
{
    $ws = new COM("WScript.Shell");
    $filename = $ws->CurrentDirectory . "\\Win32_Process.asp";
    $fso = new COM("Scripting.FileSystemObject");
    var txtstream = $fso->OpenTextFile(filename, 2, true, -2);
    $txtstream->WriteLine("<html xmlns=\"http://www.w3.org/1999/xhtml\">");
    $txtstream->WriteLine("<head>");
    $txtstream->WriteLine("<title>Win32_Process</title>");
    $txtstream->WriteLine("</head>");
    $txtstream->WriteLine("<body>");
    $txtstream->WriteLine("<%");
    $txtstream->WriteLine("Response.Write(\"<table Border=1 cellpadding=2
cellspacing=2>\" & vbcrlf)");
    $txtstream->WriteLine("Response.Write(\"<tr>\" & vbcrlf)");
    for($a=0; $a < sizeof($nd->keys);$a ++)
    {
        $txtstream->WriteLine("Response.Write(\"<th style='color:darkred;font-
size:10px;font-family:Cambria, serif;' align='left' nowrap>" . $nd->items[$a].
"</th>\" & vbcrlf)");
    }
    $txtstream->WriteLine("Response.Write(\"</tr>\" & vbcrlf)");
```

Horizontal No Additional Tags

```
for($y=0; $y < sizeof($rd->keys);$y ++)
{
  $txtstream->WriteLine("Response.Write(\"<tr>\" & vbcrlf)");
  $cd = $rd->items[$y];
  for($a=0; $a < sizeof($nd->keys);$a ++)
  {
    $txtstream->WriteLine("Response.Write(\"<td style='color:navy;font-size:10px;font-family:Cambria, serif;' align='left' nowrap>"  . $cd->items[$a] . "</td>\" & vbcrlf)");
  }
  $txtstream->WriteLine("Response.Write(\"</tr>\" & vbcrlf)");
}
```

Horizontal Using A Button

```
for($y=0; $y < sizeof($rd->keys);$y ++)
{
  $txtstream->WriteLine("Response.Write(\"<tr>\" & vbcrlf)");
  $cd = $rd->items[$y];
  for($a=0; $a < sizeof($nd->keys);$a ++)
  {
    $txtstream->WriteLine("Response.Write(\"<td style='color:navy;font-size:10px;font-family:Cambria, serif;' align='left' nowrap><input Type= button value=\"\"  . $cd->items[$a] . \"\"\"></input></td>\" & vbcrlf)");
  }
  $txtstream->WriteLine("Response.Write(\"</tr>\" & vbcrlf)");
}
```

Horizontal Using A ComboBox

```
for($y=0; $y < sizeof($rd->keys);$y ++)
```

```
{
    $txtstream->WriteLine("Response.Write(\"<tr>\" & vbcrlf)");
    $cd = $rd->items[$y];
    for($a=0; $a < sizeof($nd->keys);$a ++)
    {
        $txtstream->WriteLine("Response.Write(\"<td style='font-family:Calibri,
Sans-Serif;font-size: 12px;color:navy;' align='left' nowrap='true'><select><option
value = '" . $cd->items[$a] . "'>" . $cd->items[$a] . "</option></select></td>\" .
vbcrlf)");
    }
    $txtstream->WriteLine("Response.Write(\"</tr>\" & vbcrlf)");
}
```

Horizontal Using A Div

```
for($y=0; $y < sizeof($rd->keys);$y ++)
{
    $txtstream->WriteLine("Response.Write(\"<tr>\" & vbcrlf)");
    $cd = $rd->items[$y];
    for($a=0; $a < sizeof($nd->keys);$a ++)
    {

        $txtstream->WriteLine("Response.Write(\"<td style='color:navy;font-
size:10px;font-family:Cambria, serif;' align='left' nowrap><div>" . $cd->items[$a]
. "</div></td>\" & vbcrlf)");

    }
    $txtstream->WriteLine("Response.Write(\"</tr>\" & vbcrlf)");
}
```

Horizontal Using A Link

```
for($y=0; $y < sizeof($rd->keys);$y ++)
{
    $txtstream->WriteLine("Response.Write(\"<tr>\" & vbcrlf)");
```

```
    $cd = $rd->items[$y];
    for($a=0; $a < sizeof($nd->keys);$a ++)
    {
  $txtstream->WriteLine("Response.Write(\"<td style='font-family:Calibri, Sans-
Serif;font-size: 12px;color:navy;' align='left' nowrap='true'><a href='"  . $cd-
>items[$a] . "'>"  . $cd->items[$a] . "</a></td>\"  . vbcrlf)");
    }
    $txtstream->WriteLine("Response.Write(\"</tr>\" & vbcrlf)");
  }
```

Horizontal Using A ListBox

```
  for($y=0; $y < sizeof($rd->keys);$y ++)
  {
    $txtstream->WriteLine("Response.Write(\"<tr>\" & vbcrlf)");
    $cd = $rd->items[$y];
    for($a=0; $a < sizeof($nd->keys);$a ++)
    {
      $txtstream->WriteLine("Response.Write(\"<td style='font-family:Calibri,
Sans-Serif;font-size: 12px;color:navy;' align='left' nowrap='true'><select
multiple><option value = '"  . $cd->items[$a] . "'>"  . $cd->items[$a] .
"</option></select></td>\"  . vbcrlf)");
    }
    $txtstream->WriteLine("Response.Write(\"</tr>\" & vbcrlf)");
  }
```

Horizontal Using A Span

```
  for($y=0; $y < sizeof($rd->keys);$y ++)
  {
    $txtstream->WriteLine("Response.Write(\"<tr>\" & vbcrlf)");
    $cd = $rd->items[$y];
    for($a=0; $a < sizeof($nd->keys);$a ++)
    {
      $txtstream->WriteLine("Response.Write(\"<td style='color:navy;font-
size:10px;font-family:Cambria, serif;' align='left' nowrap><span>"  . $cd-
>items[$a] . "</span></td>\" & vbcrlf)");
```

```
    }
    $txtstream->WriteLine("Response.Write(\"</tr>\" & vbcrlf)");
}
```

Horizontal Using A Textarea

```
for($y=0; $y < sizeof($rd->keys);$y ++)
{
    $txtstream->WriteLine("Response.Write(\"<tr>\" & vbcrlf)");
    $cd = $rd->items[$y];
    for($a=0; $a < sizeof($nd->keys);$a ++)
    {
        $txtstream->WriteLine("Response.Write(\"<td style='color:navy;font-
size:10px;font-family:Cambria, serif;' align='left' nowrap><textarea>" . $cd-
>items[$a] . "</textarea></td>\" & vbcrlf)");
    }
    $txtstream->WriteLine("Response.Write(\"</tr>\" & vbcrlf)");
}
```

Horizontal Using A TextBox

```
for($y=0; $y < sizeof($rd->keys);$y ++)
{
    $txtstream->WriteLine("Response.Write(\"<tr>\" & vbcrlf)");
    $cd = $rd->items[$y];
    for($a=0; $a < sizeof($nd->keys);$a ++)
    {
        $txtstream->WriteLine("Response.Write(\"<td style='color:navy;font-
size:10px;font-family:Cambria, serif;' align='left' nowrap><input Type=text
value=\"\" . $cd->items[$a] . \"\"></input></td>\" & vbcrlf)");

    }
    $txtstream->WriteLine("Response.Write(\"</tr>\" & vbcrlf)");
}
```

Vertical No Additional Controls

```
for($a=0; $a < sizeof($nd->keys);$a ++)
{
    $txtstream->WriteLine("Response.Write(\"<tr><th style='color:darkred;font-size:10px;font-family:Cambria, serif;' align='left' nowrap>" . $nd->items[$a]. "</th>\" & vbcrlf)");
    for($y=0; $y < sizeof($rd->keys);$y ++)
    {
        $cd = $rd->items[$y];
$txtstream->WriteLine("Response.Write(\"<td style='color:navy;font-size:10px;font-family:Cambria, serif;' align='left' nowrap>" . $cd->items[$a] . "</td>\" & vbcrlf)");
    }
    $txtstream->WriteLine("Response.Write(\"</tr>\" & vbcrlf)");
}
```

Vertical Using A Button

```
for($a=0; $a < sizeof($nd->keys);$a ++)
{
    $txtstream->WriteLine("Response.Write(\"<tr><th style='color:darkred;font-size:10px;font-family:Cambria, serif;' align='left' nowrap>" . $nd->items[$a]. "</th>\" & vbcrlf)");
for($y=0; $y < sizeof($rd->keys);$y ++)
{
  $cd = $rd->items[$y];
  $txtstream->WriteLine("Response.Write(\"<td style='color:navy;font-size:10px;font-family:Cambria, serif;' align='left' nowrap><input Type= button value=\"\" . $cd->items[$a] . \"\"></input></td>\" & vbcrlf)");
}
    $txtstream->WriteLine("Response.Write(\"</tr>\" & vbcrlf)");
}
```

Vertical Using A ComboBox

```
for($a=0; $a < sizeof($nd->keys);$a ++)
{
    $txtstream->WriteLine("Response.Write(\"<tr><th style='color:darkred;font-
size:10px;font-family:Cambria, serif;' align='left' nowrap>" . $nd->items[$a].
"</th>\" & vbcrlf)");
    for($y=0; $y < sizeof($rd->keys);$y ++)
    {
        $cd = $rd->items[$y];
    $txtstream->WriteLine("Response.Write(\"<td style='font-family:Calibri, Sans-
Serif;font-size: 12px;color:navy;' align='left' nowrap='true'><select><option value =
'" . $cd->items[$a] . "'>" . $cd->items[$a] . "</option></select></td>\" .
vbcrlf)");
    }
    $txtstream->WriteLine("Response.Write(\"</tr>\" & vbcrlf)");
}
```

Vertical Using A Div

```
for($a=0; $a < sizeof($nd->keys);$a ++)
{
    $txtstream->WriteLine("Response.Write(\"<tr><th style='color:darkred;font-
size:10px;font-family:Cambria, serif;' align='left' nowrap>" . $nd->items[$a].
"</th>\" & vbcrlf)");
    for($y=0; $y < sizeof($rd->keys);$y ++)
    {
        $cd = $rd->items[$y];
    $txtstream->WriteLine("Response.Write(\"<td style='color:navy;font-
size:10px;font-family:Cambria, serif;' align='left' nowrap><div>" . $cd->items[$a]
. "</div></td>\" & vbcrlf)");
    }
    $txtstream->WriteLine("Response.Write(\"</tr>\" & vbcrlf)")
}
```

Vertical Using A Link

```
for($a=0; $a < sizeof($nd->keys);$a ++)
{
    $txtstream->WriteLine("Response.Write(\"<tr><th style='color:darkred;font-
size:10px;font-family:Cambria, serif;' align='left' nowrap>" . $nd->items[$a].
"</th>\" & vbcrlf)");
    for($y=0; $y < sizeof($rd->keys);$y ++)
    {
        $cd = $rd->items[$y];
$txtstream->WriteLine("Response.Write(\"<td style='font-family:Calibri, Sans-
Serif;font-size: 12px;color:navy;' align='left' nowrap='true'><a href='" . $cd-
>items[$a] . "'>" . $cd->items[$a] . "</a></td>\" . vbcrlf)");
    }
    $txtstream->WriteLine("Response.Write(\"</tr>\" & vbcrlf)");
}
```

Vertical Using A ListBox

```
for($a=0; $a < sizeof($nd->keys);$a ++)
{
    $txtstream->WriteLine("Response.Write(\"<tr><th style='color:darkred;font-
size:10px;font-family:Cambria, serif;' align='left' nowrap>" . $nd->items[$a].
"</th>\" & vbcrlf)");
    for($y=0; $y < sizeof($rd->keys);$y ++)
    {
        $cd = $rd->items[$y];
        $txtstream->WriteLine("Response.Write(\"<td style='font-family:Calibri,
Sans-Serif;font-size: 12px;color:navy;' align='left' nowrap='true'><select
multiple><option value = '" . $cd->items[$a] . "'>" . $cd->items[$a] .
"</option></select></td>\" . vbcrlf)");
    }
    $txtstream->WriteLine("Response.Write(\"</tr>\" & vbcrlf)");
}
```

Vertical Using A Span

```
for($a=0; $a < sizeof($nd->keys);$a ++)
```

```
    {
        $txtstream->WriteLine("Response.Write(\"<tr><th style='color:darkred;font-
size:10px;font-family:Cambria, serif;' align='left' nowrap>" . $nd->items[$a].
"</th>\" & vbcrlf)");
        for($y=0; $y < sizeof($rd->keys);$y ++)
        {
            $cd = $rd->items[$y];
    $txtstream->WriteLine("Response.Write(\"<td style='color:navy;font-
size:10px;font-family:Cambria, serif;' align='left' nowrap><span>" . $cd-
>items[$a] . "</span></td>\" & vbcrlf)");
        }
        $txtstream->WriteLine("Response.Write(\"</tr>\" & vbcrlf)");
    }
```

Vertical Using A Textarea

```
    for($a=0; $a < sizeof($nd->keys);$a ++)
    {
        $txtstream->WriteLine("Response.Write(\"<tr><th style='color:darkred;font-
size:10px;font-family:Cambria, serif;' align='left' nowrap>" . $nd->items[$a].
"</th>\" & vbcrlf)");
        for($y=0; $y < sizeof($rd->keys);$y ++)
        {
            $cd = $rd->items[$y];
    $txtstream->WriteLine("Response.Write(\"<td style='color:navy;font-
size:10px;font-family:Cambria, serif;' align='left' nowrap><textarea>" . $cd-
>items[$a] . "</textarea></td>\" & vbcrlf)");
        }
        $txtstream->WriteLine("Response.Write(\"</tr>\" & vbcrlf)");
    }
```

Vertical Using A TextBox

```
    for($a=0; $a < sizeof($nd->keys);$a ++)
    {
```

```
    $txtstream->WriteLine("Response.Write(\"<tr><th style='color:darkred;font-
size:10px;font-family:Cambria, serif;' align='left' nowrap>" . $nd->items[$a].
"</th>\" & vbcrlf)");
    for($y=0; $y < sizeof($rd->keys);$y ++)
    {
        $cd = $rd->items[$y];
  $txtstream->WriteLine("Response.Write(\"<td style='color:navy;font-
size:10px;font-family:Cambria, serif;' align='left' nowrap><input Type=text
value=\"\" . $cd->items[$a] . \"\"></input></td>\" & vbcrlf)");
    }
    $txtstream->WriteLine("Response.Write(\"</tr>\" & vbcrlf)");
  }
```

End Code

```
  $txtstream->WriteLine("Response.Write(\"</table>\" & vbcrlf)");
  $txtstream->WriteLine("%>");
  $txtstream->WriteLine("</body>");
  $txtstream->WriteLine("</html>");
  $txtstream->Close();

}
```

ASPX Reports

Begin Code

```
$ws = new COM("WScript.Shell");
$filename = $ws->CurrentDirectory . "\\Win32_Process.aspx";
$fso = new COM("Scripting.FileSystemObject");
var txtstream = $fso->OpenTextFile(filename, 2, true, -2);
$txtstream->WriteLine("<!DOCTYPE html PUBLIC \"-//W3C//DTD XHTML 1.0
Transitional//EN\" \"http://www.w3.org/TR/xhtml1/DTD/xhtml1-
transitional.dtd\">");
$txtstream->WriteLine("");
$txtstream->WriteLine("<html xmlns=\"http://www.w3.org/1999/xhtml\">");
```

```
$txtstream->WriteLine("<head>");
$txtstream->WriteLine("<title>Win32_Process</title>");
$txtstream->WriteLine("</head>");
$txtstream->WriteLine("<body>");
$txtstream->WriteLine("<%");
$txtstream->WriteLine("Response.Write(\"<table cellpadding=2 cellspacing=2>\"
& vbcrlf)");
```

Horizontal Views

```
$txtstream->WriteLine("Response.Write(\"<tr>\" & vbcrlf)");
for($a=0; $a < sizeof($nd->keys);$a ++)
{
    $txtstream->WriteLine("Response.Write(\"<th style='color:darkred;font-
size:10px;font-family:Cambria, serif;' align='left' nowrap>" . $nd->items[$a].
"</th>\" & vbcrlf)");
}
$txtstream->WriteLine("Response.Write(\"</tr>\" & vbcrlf)");
```

Horizontal No Additional Tags

```
for($y=0; $y < sizeof($rd->keys);$y ++)
{
    $txtstream->WriteLine("Response.Write(\"<tr>\" & vbcrlf)");
    $cd = $rd->items[$y];
    for($a=0; $a < sizeof($nd->keys);$a ++)
    {
        $txtstream->WriteLine("Response.Write(\"<td style='color:navy;font-
size:10px;font-family:Cambria, serif;' align='left' nowrap>" . $cd->items[$a] .
"</td>\" & vbcrlf)");
    }
    $txtstream->WriteLine("Response.Write(\"</tr>\" & vbcrlf)");
}
```

Horizontal Using A Button

```
for($y=0; $y < sizeof($rd->keys);$y ++)
{
   $txtstream->WriteLine("Response.Write(\"<tr>\" & vbcrlf)");
   $cd = $rd->items[$y];
   for($a=0; $a < sizeof($nd->keys);$a ++)
   {
      $txtstream->WriteLine("Response.Write(\"<td style='color:navy;font-
size:10px;font-family:Cambria, serif;' align='left' nowrap><input Type= button
value=\"\"  . $cd->items[$a] . \"\"></input></td>\" & vbcrlf)");
   }
   $txtstream->WriteLine("Response.Write(\"</tr>\" & vbcrlf)");
}
```

Horizontal Using A ComboBox

```
for($y=0; $y < sizeof($rd->keys);$y ++)

{

   $txtstream->WriteLine("Response.Write(\"<tr>\" & vbcrlf)");
   $cd = $rd->items[$y];
   for($a=0; $a < sizeof($nd->keys);$a ++)
   {
      $txtstream->WriteLine("Response.Write(\"<td style='font-family:Calibri,
Sans-Serif;font-size: 12px;color:navy;' align='left' nowrap='true'><select><option
value = '"  . $cd->items[$a] . "'>"  . $cd->items[$a] . "</option></select></td>\"  .
vbcrlf)");
   }
   $txtstream->WriteLine("Response.Write(\"</tr>\" & vbcrlf)");
}
```

Horizontal Using A Div

```
for($y=0; $y < sizeof($rd->keys);$y ++)
{
    $txtstream->WriteLine("Response.Write(\"<tr>\" & vbcrlf)");
    $cd = $rd->items[$y];
    for($a=0; $a < sizeof($nd->keys);$a ++)
    {

        $txtstream->WriteLine("Response.Write(\"<td style='color:navy;font-
size:10px;font-family:Cambria, serif;' align='left' nowrap><div>" . $cd->items[$a]
. "</div></td>\" & vbcrlf)");

    }
    $txtstream->WriteLine("Response.Write(\"</tr>\" & vbcrlf)");
}
```

Horizontal Using A Link

```
for($y=0; $y < sizeof($rd->keys);$y ++)
{
    $txtstream->WriteLine("Response.Write(\"<tr>\" & vbcrlf)");
    $cd = $rd->items[$y];
    for($a=0; $a < sizeof($nd->keys);$a ++)
    {
$txtstream->WriteLine("Response.Write(\"<td style='font-family:Calibri, Sans-
Serif;font-size: 12px;color:navy;' align='left' nowrap='true'><a href='" . $cd-
>items[$a] . "'>" . $cd->items[$a] . "</a></td>\" . vbcrlf)");
    }
    $txtstream->WriteLine("Response.Write(\"</tr>\" & vbcrlf)");
}
```

Horizontal Using A ListBox

```
{
```

```
for($y=0; $y < sizeof($rd->keys);$y ++)
{
    $txtstream->WriteLine("Response.Write(\"<tr>\" & vbcrlf)");
    $cd = $rd->items[$y];
    for($a=0; $a < sizeof($nd->keys);$a ++)
    {
        $txtstream->WriteLine("Response.Write(\"<td style='font-family:Calibri,
Sans-Serif;font-size: 12px;color:navy;' align='left' nowrap='true'><select
multiple><option value = '" . $cd->items[$a] . "'>" . $cd->items[$a] .
"</option></select></td>\" . vbcrlf)");
    }
    $txtstream->WriteLine("Response.Write(\"</tr>\" & vbcrlf)");
}
```

Horizontal Using A Span

```
for($y=0; $y < sizeof($rd->keys);$y ++)
{
    $txtstream->WriteLine("Response.Write(\"<tr>\" & vbcrlf)");
    $cd = $rd->items[$y];
    for($a=0; $a < sizeof($nd->keys);$a ++)
    {
        $txtstream->WriteLine("Response.Write(\"<tr>\" & vbcrlf)");

        $cd = $rd->items[$y];

        $txtstream->WriteLine("Response.Write(\"<td style='color:navy;font-
size:10px;font-family:Cambria, serif;' align='left' nowrap><span>" . $cd-
>items[$a] . "</span></td>\" & vbcrlf)");
    }
    $txtstream->WriteLine("Response.Write(\"</tr>\" & vbcrlf)");
}
```

Horizontal Using A Textarea

```
for($y=0; $y < sizeof($rd->keys);$y ++)
```

```
    {
        $txtstream->WriteLine("Response.Write(\"<tr>\" & vbcrlf)");
        $cd = $rd->items[$y];
        for($a=0; $a < sizeof($nd->keys);$a ++)
        {
            $txtstream->WriteLine("Response.Write(\"<td style='color:navy;font-
size:10px;font-family:Cambria, serif;' align='left' nowrap><textarea>" . $cd-
>items[$a] . "</textarea></td>\" & vbcrlf)");
        }
        $txtstream->WriteLine("Response.Write(\"</tr>\" & vbcrlf)");
    }
```

Horizontal Using A TextBox

```
    for($y=0; $y < sizeof($rd->keys);$y ++)
    {
        $txtstream->WriteLine("Response.Write(\"<tr>\" & vbcrlf)");
        $cd = $rd->items[$y];
        for($a=0; $a < sizeof($nd->keys);$a ++)
        {
            $txtstream->WriteLine("Response.Write(\"<td style='color:navy;font-
size:10px;font-family:Cambria, serif;' align='left' nowrap><input Type=text
value=\"\" . $cd->items[$a] . \"\"></input></td>\" & vbcrlf)");

        }
        $txtstream->WriteLine("Response.Write(\"</tr>\" & vbcrlf)");
    }
```

Vertical No Additional Controls

```
    for($a=0; $a < sizeof($nd->keys);$a ++)
    {
        $txtstream->WriteLine("Response.Write(\"<tr><th style='color:darkred;font-
size:10px;font-family:Cambria, serif;' align='left' nowrap>" . $nd->items[$a].
"</th>\" & vbcrlf)");
        for($y=0; $y < sizeof($rd->keys);$y ++)
```

```
    {
        $cd = $rd->items[$y];
    $txtstream->WriteLine("Response.Write(\"<td style='color:navy;font-
size:10px;font-family:Cambria, serif;' align='left' nowrap>" . $cd->items[$a] .
"</td>\" & vbcrlf)");
    }
        $txtstream->WriteLine("Response.Write(\"</tr>\" & vbcrlf)");
    }
```

Vertical Using A Button

```
    for($a=0; $a < sizeof($nd->keys);$a ++)
    {
        $txtstream->WriteLine("Response.Write(\"<tr><th style='color:darkred;font-
size:10px;font-family:Cambria, serif;' align='left' nowrap>" . $nd->items[$a].
"</th>\" & vbcrlf)");
for($y=0; $y < sizeof($rd->keys);$y ++)
{
    $cd = $rd->items[$y];
    $txtstream->WriteLine("Response.Write(\"<td style='color:navy;font-
size:10px;font-family:Cambria, serif;' align='left' nowrap><input Type= button
value=\"\" . $cd->items[$a] . \"\"></input></td>\" & vbcrlf)");
}
        $txtstream->WriteLine("Response.Write(\"</tr>\" & vbcrlf)");
    }
```

Vertical Using A ComboBox

```
    for($a=0; $a < sizeof($nd->keys);$a ++)
    {
        $txtstream->WriteLine("Response.Write(\"<tr><th style='color:darkred;font-
size:10px;font-family:Cambria, serif;' align='left' nowrap>" . $nd->items[$a].
"</th>\" & vbcrlf)");
        for($y=0; $y < sizeof($rd->keys);$y ++)
        {
            $cd = $rd->items[$y];
```

```
    $txtstream->WriteLine("Response.Write(\"<td style='font-family:Calibri, Sans-
Serif;font-size: 12px;color:navy;' align='left' nowrap='true'><select><option value =
'" . $cd->items[$a] . "'>" . $cd->items[$a] . "</option></select></td>\" .
vbcrlf)");
    }
    $txtstream->WriteLine("Response.Write(\"</tr>\" & vbcrlf)");
  }
```

Vertical Using A Div

```
  for($a=0; $a < sizeof($nd->keys);$a ++)
  {
    $txtstream->WriteLine("Response.Write(\"<tr><th style='color:darkred;font-
size:10px;font-family:Cambria, serif;' align='left' nowrap>" . $nd->items[$a].
"</th>\" & vbcrlf)");
    for($y=0; $y < sizeof($rd->keys);$y ++)
    {
      $cd = $rd->items[$y];
  $txtstream->WriteLine("Response.Write(\"<td style='color:navy;font-
size:10px;font-family:Cambria, serif;' align='left' nowrap><div>" . $cd->items[$a]
. "</div></td>\" & vbcrlf)");
    }
    $txtstream->WriteLine("Response.Write(\"</tr>\" & vbcrlf)")
  }
```

Vertical Using A Link

```
  for($a=0; $a < sizeof($nd->keys);$a ++)
  {
    $txtstream->WriteLine("Response.Write(\"<tr><th style='color:darkred;font-
size:10px;font-family:Cambria, serif;' align='left' nowrap>" . $nd->items[$a].
"</th>\" & vbcrlf)");
    for($y=0; $y < sizeof($rd->keys);$y ++)
    {
      $cd = $rd->items[$y];
```

```
$txtstream->WriteLine("Response.Write(\"<td style='font-family:Calibri, Sans-
Serif;font-size: 12px;color:navy;' align='left' nowrap='true'><a href='" . $cd-
>items[$a] . "'>" . $cd->items[$a] . "</a></td>\" . vbcrlf)");
    }
    $txtstream->WriteLine("Response.Write(\"</tr>\" & vbcrlf)");
  }
```

Vertical Using A ListBox

```
  for($a=0; $a < sizeof($nd->keys);$a ++)
  {
    $txtstream->WriteLine("Response.Write(\"<tr><th style='color:darkred;font-
size:10px;font-family:Cambria, serif;' align='left' nowrap>" . $nd->items[$a].
"</th>\" & vbcrlf)");
    for($y=0; $y < sizeof($rd->keys);$y ++)
    {
      $cd = $rd->items[$y];
      $txtstream->WriteLine("Response.Write(\"<td style='font-family:Calibri,
Sans-Serif;font-size: 12px;color:navy;' align='left' nowrap='true'><select
multiple><option value = '" . $cd->items[$a] . "'>" . $cd->items[$a] .
"</option></select></td>\" . vbcrlf)");
    }
    $txtstream->WriteLine("Response.Write(\"</tr>\" & vbcrlf)");
  }
```

Vertical Using A Span

```
  for($a=0; $a < sizeof($nd->keys);$a ++)
  {
    $txtstream->WriteLine("Response.Write(\"<tr><th style='color:darkred;font-
size:10px;font-family:Cambria, serif;' align='left' nowrap>" . $nd->items[$a].
"</th>\" & vbcrlf)");
    for($y=0; $y < sizeof($rd->keys);$y ++)
    {
      $cd = $rd->items[$y];
  $txtstream->WriteLine("Response.Write(\"<td style='color:navy;font-
size:10px;font-family:Cambria, serif;' align='left' nowrap><span>" . $cd-
>items[$a] . "</span></td>\" & vbcrlf)");
```

```
        }
    $txtstream->WriteLine("Response.Write(\"</tr>\" & vbcrlf)");
  }
```

Vertical Using A Textarea

```
    for($a=0; $a < sizeof($nd->keys);$a ++)
    {
        $txtstream->WriteLine("Response.Write(\"<tr><th style='color:darkred;font-size:10px;font-family:Cambria, serif;' align='left' nowrap>" . $nd->items[$a]. "</th>\" & vbcrlf)");
        for($y=0; $y < sizeof($rd->keys);$y ++)
        {
            $cd = $rd->items[$y];
    $txtstream->WriteLine("Response.Write(\"<td style='color:navy;font-size:10px;font-family:Cambria, serif;' align='left' nowrap><textarea>" . $cd->items[$a] . "</textarea></td>\" & vbcrlf)");
        }
        $txtstream->WriteLine("Response.Write(\"</tr>\" & vbcrlf)");
  }
```

Vertical Using A TextBox

```
    for($a=0; $a < sizeof($nd->keys);$a ++)
    {
        $txtstream->WriteLine("Response.Write(\"<tr><th style='color:darkred;font-size:10px;font-family:Cambria, serif;' align='left' nowrap>" . $nd->items[$a]. "</th>\" & vbcrlf)");
        for($y=0; $y < sizeof($rd->keys);$y ++)
        {
            $cd = $rd->items[$y];
    $txtstream->WriteLine("Response.Write(\"<td style='color:navy;font-size:10px;font-family:Cambria, serif;' align='left' nowrap><input Type=text value=\"\" . $cd->items[$a] . \"\"></input></td>\" & vbcrlf)");
        }
        $txtstream->WriteLine("Response.Write(\"</tr>\" & vbcrlf)");
  }
```

End Code

```
$txtstream->WriteLine("Response.Write(\"</table>\" & vbcrlf)");
$txtstream->WriteLine("%>");
$txtstream->WriteLine("</body>");
$txtstream->WriteLine("</html>");
$txtstream->Close();

}
```

Begin Code

```
function Write_The_Code()
{
   $ws = new COM("WScript.Shell");
   $filename = $ws->CurrentDirectory . "\\Win32_Process.aspx";
   $fso = new COM("Scripting.FileSystemObject");
   var txtstream = $fso->OpenTextFile(filename, 2, true, -2);
   $txtstream->WriteLine("<html xmlns=\"http://www.w3.org/1999/xhtml\">");
   $txtstream->WriteLine("<head>");
   $txtstream->WriteLine("<title>Win32_Process</title>");
   $txtstream->WriteLine("</head>");
   $txtstream->WriteLine("<body>");
   $txtstream->WriteLine("<%");
   $txtstream->WriteLine("Response.Write(\"<table cellpadding=2 cellspacing=2>\"
& vbcrlf)");
   $txtstream->WriteLine("Response.Write(\"<tr>\" & vbcrlf)");
   for($a=0; $a < sizeof($nd->keys);$a ++)
   {
      $txtstream->WriteLine("Response.Write(\"<th style='color:darkred;font-
size:10px;font-family:Cambria, serif;' align='left' nowrap>" . $nd->items[$a].
"</th>\" & vbcrlf)");
   }
   $txtstream->WriteLine("Response.Write(\"</tr>\" & vbcrlf)");
```

Horizontal No Additional Tags

```
   for($y=0; $y < sizeof($rd->keys);$y ++)
```

```
    {
        $txtstream->WriteLine("Response.Write(\"<tr>\" & vbcrlf)");
        $cd = $rd->items[$y];
        for($a=0; $a < sizeof($nd->keys);$a ++)
        {
            $txtstream->WriteLine("Response.Write(\"<td style='color:navy;font-
size:10px;font-family:Cambria, serif;' align='left' nowrap>" . $cd->items[$a] .
"</td>\" & vbcrlf)");
        }
        $txtstream->WriteLine("Response.Write(\"</tr>\" & vbcrlf)");
    }
```

Horizontal Using A Button

```
    for($y=0; $y < sizeof($rd->keys);$y ++)
    {
        $txtstream->WriteLine("Response.Write(\"<tr>\" & vbcrlf)");
        $cd = $rd->items[$y];
        for($a=0; $a < sizeof($nd->keys);$a ++)
        {
            $txtstream->WriteLine("Response.Write(\"<td style='color:navy;font-
size:10px;font-family:Cambria, serif;' align='left' nowrap><input Type= button
value=\"\" . $cd->items[$a] . \"\"></input></td>\" & vbcrlf)");
        }
        $txtstream->WriteLine("Response.Write(\"</tr>\" & vbcrlf)");
    }
```

Horizontal Using A ComboBox

```
    for($y=0; $y < sizeof($rd->keys);$y ++)

    {

        $txtstream->WriteLine("Response.Write(\"<tr>\" & vbcrlf)");
        $cd = $rd->items[$y];
        for($a=0; $a < sizeof($nd->keys);$a ++)
        {
```

```
    $txtstream->WriteLine("Response.Write(\"<td style='font-family:Calibri,
Sans-Serif;font-size: 12px;color:navy;' align='left' nowrap='true'><select><option
value = '"  . $cd->items[$a] . "'>"  . $cd->items[$a] . "</option></select></td>\"  .
vbcrlf)");
    }
    $txtstream->WriteLine("Response.Write(\"</tr>\" & vbcrlf)");
  }
```

Horizontal Using A Div

```
  for($y=0; $y < sizeof($rd->keys);$y ++)
  {
    $txtstream->WriteLine("Response.Write(\"<tr>\" & vbcrlf)");
    $cd = $rd->items[$y];
    for($a=0; $a < sizeof($nd->keys);$a ++)
    {

       $txtstream->WriteLine("Response.Write(\"<td style='color:navy;font-
size:10px;font-family:Cambria, serif;' align='left' nowrap><div>"  . $cd->items[$a]
. "</div></td>\" & vbcrlf)");

    }
    $txtstream->WriteLine("Response.Write(\"</tr>\" & vbcrlf)");
  }
```

Horizontal Using A Link

```
  for($y=0; $y < sizeof($rd->keys);$y ++)
  {
    $txtstream->WriteLine("Response.Write(\"<tr>\" & vbcrlf)");
    $cd = $rd->items[$y];
    for($a=0; $a < sizeof($nd->keys);$a ++)
    {
  $txtstream->WriteLine("Response.Write(\"<td style='font-family:Calibri, Sans-
Serif;font-size: 12px;color:navy;' align='left' nowrap='true'><a href='"  . $cd-
>items[$a] . "'>"  . $cd->items[$a] . "</a></td>\"  . vbcrlf)");
    }
```

```
    $txtstream->WriteLine("Response.Write(\"</tr>\" & vbcrlf)");
  }
```

Horizontal Using A ListBox

```
  for($y=0; $y < sizeof($rd->keys);$y ++)
  {
    $txtstream->WriteLine("Response.Write(\"<tr>\" & vbcrlf)");
    $cd = $rd->items[$y];
    for($a=0; $a < sizeof($nd->keys);$a ++)
    {
      $txtstream->WriteLine("Response.Write(\"<td style='font-family:Calibri,
Sans-Serif;font-size: 12px;color:navy;' align='left' nowrap='true'><select
multiple><option value = '"  . $cd->items[$a] . "'>" . $cd->items[$a] .
"</option></select></td>\"  . vbcrlf)");
    }
    $txtstream->WriteLine("Response.Write(\"</tr>\" & vbcrlf)");
  }
```

Horizontal Using A Span

```
  for($y=0; $y < sizeof($rd->keys);$y ++)
  {
    $txtstream->WriteLine("Response.Write(\"<tr>\" & vbcrlf)");
    $cd = $rd->items[$y];
    for($a=0; $a < sizeof($nd->keys);$a ++)
    {
      $txtstream->WriteLine("Response.Write(\"<td style='color:navy;font-
size:10px;font-family:Cambria, serif;' align='left' nowrap><span>" . $cd-
>items[$a] . "</span></td>\" & vbcrlf)");
    }
    $txtstream->WriteLine("Response.Write(\"</tr>\" & vbcrlf)");
  }
```

Horizontal Using A Textarea

```
for($y=0; $y < sizeof($rd->keys);$y ++)
{
    $txtstream->WriteLine("Response.Write(\"<tr>\" & vbcrlf)");
    $cd = $rd->items[$y];
    for($a=0; $a < sizeof($nd->keys);$a ++)
    {
        $txtstream->WriteLine("Response.Write(\"<td style='color:navy;font-
size:10px;font-family:Cambria, serif;' align='left' nowrap><textarea>" . $cd-
>items[$a] . "</textarea></td>\" & vbcrlf)");
    }
    $txtstream->WriteLine("Response.Write(\"</tr>\" & vbcrlf)");
}
```

Horizontal Using A TextBox

```
for($y=0; $y < sizeof($rd->keys);$y ++)
{
    $txtstream->WriteLine("Response.Write(\"<tr>\" & vbcrlf)");
    $cd = $rd->items[$y];
    for($a=0; $a < sizeof($nd->keys);$a ++)
    {
        $txtstream->WriteLine("Response.Write(\"<td style='color:navy;font-
size:10px;font-family:Cambria, serif;' align='left' nowrap><input Type=text
value=\"\" . $cd->items[$a] . \"\"></input></td>\" & vbcrlf)");

    }
    $txtstream->WriteLine("Response.Write(\"</tr>\" & vbcrlf)");
}
```

Vertical No Additional Controls

```
for($a=0; $a < sizeof($nd->keys);$a ++)
{
    $txtstream->WriteLine("Response.Write(\"<tr><th style='color:darkred;font-
size:10px;font-family:Cambria, serif;' align='left' nowrap>" . $nd->items[$a].
"</th>\" & vbcrlf)");
```

```
    for($y=0; $y < sizeof($rd->keys);$y ++)
    {
        $cd = $rd->items[$y];
$txtstream->WriteLine("Response.Write(\"<td style='color:navy;font-
size:10px;font-family:Cambria, serif;' align='left' nowrap>" . $cd->items[$a] .
"</td>\" & vbcrlf)");
    }
    $txtstream->WriteLine("Response.Write(\"</tr>\" & vbcrlf)");
}
```

Vertical Using A Button

```
    for($a=0; $a < sizeof($nd->keys);$a ++)
    {
        $txtstream->WriteLine("Response.Write(\"<tr><th style='color:darkred;font-
size:10px;font-family:Cambria, serif;' align='left' nowrap>" . $nd->items[$a].
"</th>\" & vbcrlf)");
for($y=0; $y < sizeof($rd->keys);$y ++)
{
    $cd = $rd->items[$y];
    $txtstream->WriteLine("Response.Write(\"<td style='color:navy;font-
size:10px;font-family:Cambria, serif;' align='left' nowrap><input Type= button
value=\"\" . $cd->items[$a] . \"\"></input></td>\" & vbcrlf)");
}
        $txtstream->WriteLine("Response.Write(\"</tr>\" & vbcrlf)");
    }
```

Vertical Using A ComboBox

```
    for($a=0; $a < sizeof($nd->keys);$a ++)
    {
        $txtstream->WriteLine("Response.Write(\"<tr><th style='color:darkred;font-
size:10px;font-family:Cambria, serif;' align='left' nowrap>" . $nd->items[$a].
"</th>\" & vbcrlf)");
        for($y=0; $y < sizeof($rd->keys);$y ++)
        {
```

```
        $cd = $rd->items[$y];
  $txtstream->WriteLine("Response.Write(\"<td style='font-family:Calibri, Sans-
Serif;font-size: 12px;color:navy;' align='left' nowrap='true'><select><option value =
'" . $cd->items[$a] . "'>" . $cd->items[$a] . "</option></select></td>\" .
vbcrlf)");
      }
      $txtstream->WriteLine("Response.Write(\"</tr>\" & vbcrlf)");
  }
```

Vertical Using A Div

```
  for($a=0; $a < sizeof($nd->keys);$a ++)
  {
      $txtstream->WriteLine("Response.Write(\"<tr><th style='color:darkred;font-
size:10px;font-family:Cambria, serif;' align='left' nowrap>" . $nd->items[$a].
"</th>\" & vbcrlf)");
      for($y=0; $y < sizeof($rd->keys);$y ++)
      {
          $cd = $rd->items[$y];
  $txtstream->WriteLine("Response.Write(\"<td style='color:navy;font-
size:10px;font-family:Cambria, serif;' align='left' nowrap><div>" . $cd->items[$a]
. "</div></td>\" & vbcrlf)");
      }
      $txtstream->WriteLine("Response.Write(\"</tr>\" & vbcrlf)")
  }
```

Vertical Using A Link

```
  for($a=0; $a < sizeof($nd->keys);$a ++)
  {
      $txtstream->WriteLine("Response.Write(\"<tr><th style='color:darkred;font-
size:10px;font-family:Cambria, serif;' align='left' nowrap>" . $nd->items[$a].
"</th>\" & vbcrlf)");
      for($y=0; $y < sizeof($rd->keys);$y ++)
      {
          $cd = $rd->items[$y];
```

```
$txtstream->WriteLine("Response.Write(\"<td style='font-family:Calibri, Sans-
Serif;font-size: 12px;color:navy;' align='left' nowrap='true'><a href='" . $cd-
>items[$a] . "'>" . $cd->items[$a] . "</a></td>\" . vbcrlf)");
      }
      $txtstream->WriteLine("Response.Write(\"</tr>\" & vbcrlf)");
  }
```

Vertical Using A ListBox

```
  for($a=0; $a < sizeof($nd->keys);$a ++)
  {
      $txtstream->WriteLine("Response.Write(\"<tr><th style='color:darkred;font-
size:10px;font-family:Cambria, serif;' align='left' nowrap>" . $nd->items[$a].
"</th>\" & vbcrlf)");
      for($y=0; $y < sizeof($rd->keys);$y ++)
      {
        $cd = $rd->items[$y];
        $txtstream->WriteLine("Response.Write(\"<td style='font-family:Calibri,
Sans-Serif;font-size: 12px;color:navy;' align='left' nowrap='true'><select
multiple><option value = '" . $cd->items[$a] . "'>" . $cd->items[$a] .
"</option></select></td>\" . vbcrlf)");
      }
      $txtstream->WriteLine("Response.Write(\"</tr>\" & vbcrlf)");
  }
```

Vertical Using A Span

```
  for($a=0; $a < sizeof($nd->keys);$a ++)
  {
      $txtstream->WriteLine("Response.Write(\"<tr><th style='color:darkred;font-
size:10px;font-family:Cambria, serif;' align='left' nowrap>" . $nd->items[$a].
"</th>\" & vbcrlf)");
      for($y=0; $y < sizeof($rd->keys);$y ++)
      {
        $cd = $rd->items[$y];
    $txtstream->WriteLine("Response.Write(\"<td style='color:navy;font-
size:10px;font-family:Cambria, serif;' align='left' nowrap><span>" . $cd-
>items[$a] . "</span></td>\" & vbcrlf)");
```

```
    }
    $txtstream->WriteLine("Response.Write(\"</tr>\" & vbcrlf)");
  }
```

Vertical Using A Textarea

```
  for($a=0; $a < sizeof($nd->keys);$a ++)
  {
      $txtstream->WriteLine("Response.Write(\"<tr><th style='color:darkred;font-
size:10px;font-family:Cambria, serif;' align='left' nowrap>" . $nd->items[$a].
"</th>\" & vbcrlf)");
      for($y=0; $y < sizeof($rd->keys);$y ++)
      {
          $cd = $rd->items[$y];
  $txtstream->WriteLine("Response.Write(\"<td style='color:navy;font-
size:10px;font-family:Cambria, serif;' align='left' nowrap><textarea>" . $cd-
>items[$a] . "</textarea></td>\" & vbcrlf)");
      }
      $txtstream->WriteLine("Response.Write(\"</tr>\" & vbcrlf)");
  }
```

Vertical Using A TextBox

```
  for($a=0; $a < sizeof($nd->keys);$a ++)
  {
      $txtstream->WriteLine("Response.Write(\"<tr><th style='color:darkred;font-
size:10px;font-family:Cambria, serif;' align='left' nowrap>" . $nd->items[$a].
"</th>\" & vbcrlf)");
      for($y=0; $y < sizeof($rd->keys);$y ++)
      {
          $cd = $rd->items[$y];
  $txtstream->WriteLine("Response.Write(\"<td style='color:navy;font-
size:10px;font-family:Cambria, serif;' align='left' nowrap><input Type=text
value=\"\" . $cd->items[$a] . \"\"></input></td>\" & vbcrlf)");
      }
      $txtstream->WriteLine("Response.Write(\"</tr>\" & vbcrlf)");
  }
```

End Code

```
$txtstream->WriteLine("Response.Write(\"</table>\" & vbcrlf)");
$txtstream->WriteLine("%>");
$txtstream->WriteLine("</body>");
$txtstream->WriteLine("</html>");
$txtstream->Close();

}
```

Begin Code

```
function Write_The_Code()
{

    $ws = new COM("WScript.Shell");
    $filename = $ws->CurrentDirectory . "\\Win32_Process.hta";
    $fso = new COM("Scripting.FileSystemObject");
    var txtstream = $fso->OpenTextFile(filename, 2, true, -2);
    $txtstream->WriteLine("<html>");
    $txtstream->WriteLine("<head>");
    $txtstream->WriteLine("<HTA:APPLICATION ");
    $txtstream->WriteLine(" ID = \"Win32_Process\" ");
    $txtstream->WriteLine(" APPLICATIONNAME = \"Win32_Process\" ");
    $txtstream->WriteLine(" SCROLL = \"Yes\" ");
    $txtstream->WriteLine(" SINGLEINSTANCE = \"yes\" ");
    $txtstream->WriteLine(" WINDOWSTATE = \"normal\">");
    $txtstream->WriteLine("<title>Win32_Process</title>");
    $txtstream->WriteLine("</head>");
    $txtstream->WriteLine("<body>");
    $txtstream->WriteLine("<table  boder=0 cellpadding=2 cellspacing=2>\" &
vbcrlf)");
```

Horizontal No Additional Tags

```
for($y=0; $y < sizeof($rd->keys);$y ++)
{
    $txtstream->WriteLine("<tr>\" & vbcrlf)");
    $cd = $rd->items[$y];
    for($a=0; $a < sizeof($nd->keys);$a ++)
    {
        $txtstream->WriteLine("<td style='color:navy;font-size:10px;font-
family:Cambria, serif;' align='left' nowrap>" . $cd->items[$a] . "</td>");
    }
    $txtstream->WriteLine("</tr>");
}
```

Horizontal Using A Button

```
for($y=0; $y < sizeof($rd->keys);$y ++)
{
    $txtstream->WriteLine("<tr>");
    $cd = $rd->items[$y];
    for($a=0; $a < sizeof($nd->keys);$a ++)
    {
        $txtstream->WriteLine("<td style='color:navy;font-size:10px;font-
family:Cambria, serif;' align='left' nowrap><input Type= button value=\"\" . $cd-
>items[$a] . \"\"></input></td>");
    }
    $txtstream->WriteLine("</tr>");
}
```

Horizontal Using A ComboBox

```
for($y=0; $y < sizeof($rd->keys);$y ++)

{
```

```
    $txtstream->WriteLine("<tr>");
    $cd = $rd->items[$y];
    for($a=0; $a < sizeof($nd->keys);$a ++)
    {
        $txtstream->WriteLine("<td style='font-family:Calibri, Sans-Serif;font-size:
12px;color:navy;' align='left' nowrap='true'><select><option value = '" . $cd-
>items[$a] . "'>" . $cd->items[$a] . "</option></select></td>\" . vbcrlf)");
    }
    $txtstream->WriteLine("</tr>");
  }
```

Horizontal Using A Div

```
  for($y=0; $y < sizeof($rd->keys);$y ++)
  {
    $txtstream->WriteLine("<tr>");
    $cd = $rd->items[$y];
    for($a=0; $a < sizeof($nd->keys);$a ++)
    {

        $txtstream->WriteLine("<td style='color:navy;font-size:10px;font-
family:Cambria, serif;' align='left' nowrap><div>" . $cd->items[$a] .
"</div></td>");

    }
    $txtstream->WriteLine("</tr>");
  }
```

Horizontal Using A Link

```
  for($y=0; $y < sizeof($rd->keys);$y ++)
  {
    $txtstream->WriteLine("<tr>");
    $cd = $rd->items[$y];
    for($a=0; $a < sizeof($nd->keys);$a ++)
```

```
        {
    $txtstream->WriteLine("<td style='font-family:Calibri, Sans-Serif;font-size:
12px;color:navy;' align='left' nowrap='true'><a href='"  . $cd->items[$a] . "'>"  .
$cd->items[$a] . "</a></td>\"  . vbcrlf)");
        }
    $txtstream->WriteLine("</tr>");
    }
```

Horizontal Using A ListBox

```
    for($y=0; $y < sizeof($rd->keys);$y ++)
    {
        $txtstream->WriteLine("Response.Write(\"<tr>\" & vbcrlf)");
        $cd = $rd->items[$y];
        for($a=0; $a < sizeof($nd->keys);$a ++)
        {
            $txtstream->WriteLine("<td style='font-family:Calibri, Sans-Serif;font-size:
12px;color:navy;' align='left' nowrap='true'><select multiple><option value = '"  .
$cd->items[$a] . "'>"  . $cd->items[$a] . "</option></select></td>\"  . vbcrlf)");
        }
        $txtstream->WriteLine("</tr>");
    }
```

Horizontal Using A Span

```
    for($y=0; $y < sizeof($rd->keys);$y ++)
    {
        $txtstream->WriteLine("Response.Write(\"<tr>\" & vbcrlf)");
        $cd = $rd->items[$y];
        for($a=0; $a < sizeof($nd->keys);$a ++)
        {
            $txtstream->WriteLine("<td style='color:navy;font-size:10px;font-
family:Cambria, serif;' align='left' nowrap><span>"  . $cd->items[$a] .
"</span></td>");
        }
        $txtstream->WriteLine("</tr>");
    }
```

Horizontal Using A Textarea

```
for($y=0; $y < sizeof($rd->keys);$y ++)
{
   $txtstream->WriteLine("Response.Write(\"<tr>\" & vbcrlf)");
   $cd = $rd->items[$y];
   for($a=0; $a < sizeof($nd->keys);$a ++)
   {
      $txtstream->WriteLine("<td style='color:navy;font-size:10px;font-
family:Cambria, serif;' align='left' nowrap><textarea>" . $cd->items[$a] .
"</textarea></td>");
   }
   $txtstream->WriteLine("</tr>");
}
```

Horizontal Using A TextBox

```
for($y=0; $y < sizeof($rd->keys);$y ++)
{
   $txtstream->WriteLine("Response.Write(\"<tr>\" & vbcrlf)");
   $cd = $rd->items[$y];
   for($a=0; $a < sizeof($nd->keys);$a ++)
   {
      $txtstream->WriteLine("<td style='color:navy;font-size:10px;font-
family:Cambria, serif;' align='left' nowrap><input Type=text value=\"\" . $cd-
>items[$a] . \"\"></input></td>");

   }
   $txtstream->WriteLine("</tr>");
}
```

Vertical No Additional Controls

```
for($a=0; $a < sizeof($nd->keys);$a ++)
{
   $txtstream->WriteLine("<tr><th style='color:darkred;font-size:10px;font-
family:Cambria, serif;' align='left' nowrap>" . $nd->items[$a]. "</th>");
   for($y=0; $y < sizeof($rd->keys);$y ++)
   {
      $cd = $rd->items[$y];
$txtstream->WriteLine("<td style='color:navy;font-size:10px;font-
family:Cambria, serif;' align='left' nowrap>" . $cd->items[$a] . "</td>");
   }
   $txtstream->WriteLine("</tr>");
}
```

Vertical Using A Button

```
for($a=0; $a < sizeof($nd->keys);$a ++)
{
   $txtstream->WriteLine("<tr><th style='color:darkred;font-size:10px;font-
family:Cambria, serif;' align='left' nowrap>" . $nd->items[$a]. "</th>");
for($y=0; $y < sizeof($rd->keys);$y ++)
{
  $cd = $rd->items[$y];
   $txtstream->WriteLine("<td style='color:navy;font-size:10px;font-
family:Cambria, serif;' align='left' nowrap><input Type= button value=\"\" . $cd-
>items[$a] . \"\"></input></td>");
}
   $txtstream->WriteLine("</tr>");
}
```

Vertical Using A ComboBox

```
for($a=0; $a < sizeof($nd->keys);$a ++)
```

```
    {
        $txtstream->WriteLine("<tr><th style='color:darkred;font-size:10px;font-
family:Cambria, serif;' align='left' nowrap>" . $nd->items[$a]. "</th>");
        for($y=0; $y < sizeof($rd->keys);$y ++)
        {
            $cd = $rd->items[$y];
    $txtstream->WriteLine("<td style='font-family:Calibri, Sans-Serif;font-size:
12px;color:navy;' align='left' nowrap='true'><select><option value = '" . $cd-
>items[$a] . "'>" . $cd->items[$a] . "</option></select></td>\" . vbcrlf)");
        }
        $txtstream->WriteLine("</tr>");
    }
```

Vertical Using A Div

```
    for($a=0; $a < sizeof($nd->keys);$a ++)
    {
        $txtstream->WriteLine("<tr><th style='color:darkred;font-size:10px;font-
family:Cambria, serif;' align='left' nowrap>" . $nd->items[$a]. "</th>");
        for($y=0; $y < sizeof($rd->keys);$y ++)
        {
            $cd = $rd->items[$y];
    $txtstream->WriteLine("<td style='color:navy;font-size:10px;font-
family:Cambria, serif;' align='left' nowrap><div>" . $cd->items[$a] .
"</div></td>");
        }
        $txtstream->WriteLine("</tr>")
    }
```

Vertical Using A Link

```
    for($a=0; $a < sizeof($nd->keys);$a ++)
    {
        $txtstream->WriteLine("<tr><th style='color:darkred;font-size:10px;font-
family:Cambria, serif;' align='left' nowrap>" . $nd->items[$a]. "</th>");
        for($y=0; $y < sizeof($rd->keys);$y ++)
        {
```

```
        $cd = $rd->items[$y];
    $txtstream->WriteLine("<td style='font-family:Calibri, Sans-Serif;font-size:
12px;color:navy;' align='left' nowrap='true'><a href='"  . $cd->items[$a] . "'>" .
$cd->items[$a] . "</a></td>\"  . vbcrlf)");
        }
        $txtstream->WriteLine("</tr>");
    }
```

Vertical Using A ListBox

```
    for($a=0; $a < sizeof($nd->keys);$a ++)
    {
        $txtstream->WriteLine("<tr><th style='color:darkred;font-size:10px;font-
family:Cambria, serif;' align='left' nowrap>" . $nd->items[$a]. "</th>");
        for($y=0; $y < sizeof($rd->keys);$y ++)
        {
            $cd = $rd->items[$y];
        $txtstream->WriteLine("<td style='font-family:Calibri, Sans-Serif;font-size:
12px;color:navy;' align='left' nowrap='true'><select multiple><option value = '"  .
$cd->items[$a] . "'>" . $cd->items[$a] . "</option></select></td>\"  . vbcrlf)");
        }
        $txtstream->WriteLine("</tr>");
    }
```

Vertical Using A Span

```
    for($a=0; $a < sizeof($nd->keys);$a ++)
    {
        $txtstream->WriteLine("<tr><th style='color:darkred;font-size:10px;font-
family:Cambria, serif;' align='left' nowrap>" . $nd->items[$a]. "</th>");
        for($y=0; $y < sizeof($rd->keys);$y ++)
        {
            $cd = $rd->items[$y];
    $txtstream->WriteLine("<td style='color:navy;font-size:10px;font-
family:Cambria, serif;' align='left' nowrap><span>" . $cd->items[$a] .
"</span></td>");
        }
        $txtstream->WriteLine("</tr>");
```

```
      }
```

Vertical Using A Textarea

```
  for($a=0; $a < sizeof($nd->keys);$a ++)
  {
      $txtstream->WriteLine("<tr><th style='color:darkred;font-size:10px;font-
family:Cambria, serif;' align='left' nowrap>" . $nd->items[$a]. "</th>");
      for($y=0; $y < sizeof($rd->keys);$y ++)
      {
         $cd = $rd->items[$y];
   $txtstream->WriteLine("<td style='color:navy;font-size:10px;font-
family:Cambria, serif;' align='left' nowrap><textarea>" . $cd->items[$a] .
"</textarea></td>");
      }
      $txtstream->WriteLine("</tr>");
   }
```

Vertical Using A TextBox

```
  for($a=0; $a < sizeof($nd->keys);$a ++)
  {
      $txtstream->WriteLine("<tr><th style='color:darkred;font-size:10px;font-
family:Cambria, serif;' align='left' nowrap>" . $nd->items[$a]. "</th>");
      for($y=0; $y < sizeof($rd->keys);$y ++)
      {
         $cd = $rd->items[$y];
   $txtstream->WriteLine("<td style='color:navy;font-size:10px;font-
family:Cambria, serif;' align='left' nowrap><input Type=text value=\"\" . $cd-
>items[$a] . \"\"></input></td>");
      }
      $txtstream->WriteLine("</tr>");
   }
```

End Code

```
    $txtstream->WriteLine("</table>");
    $txtstream->WriteLine("</body>");
    $txtstream->WriteLine("</html>");
    $txtstream->Close();
}
```

HTA TABLES

```
function Write_The_Code()
{

    $ws = new COM("WScript.Shell");
    $filename = $ws->CurrentDirectory . "\\Win32_Process.hta";
    $fso = new COM("Scripting.FileSystemObject");
    var txtstream = $fso->OpenTextFile(filename, 2, true, -2);
    $txtstream->WriteLine("<html>");
    $txtstream->WriteLine("<head>");
    $txtstream->WriteLine("<HTA:APPLICATION ");
    $txtstream->WriteLine(" ID = \"Win32_Process\" ");
    $txtstream->WriteLine(" APPLICATIONNAME = \"Win32_Process\" ");
    $txtstream->WriteLine(" SCROLL = \"Yes\" ");
    $txtstream->WriteLine(" SINGLEINSTANCE = \"yes\" ");
    $txtstream->WriteLine(" WINDOWSTATE = \"normal\">");
    $txtstream->WriteLine("<title>Win32_Process</title>");
    $txtstream->WriteLine("</head>");
    $txtstream->WriteLine("<body>");
    $txtstream->WriteLine("<table  boder=1 cellpadding=2 cellspacing=2>");
```

Horizontal No Additional Tags

```
for($y=0; $y < sizeof($rd->keys);$y ++)
{
   $txtstream->WriteLine("<tr>");
   $cd = $rd->items[$y];
   for($a=0; $a < sizeof($nd->keys);$a ++)
   {
      $txtstream->WriteLine("<td style='color:navy;font-size:10px;font-
family:Cambria, serif;' align='left' nowrap>" . $cd->items[$a] . "</td>");
   }
   $txtstream->WriteLine("</tr>");
}
```

Horizontal Using A Button

```
for($y=0; $y < sizeof($rd->keys);$y ++)
{
   $txtstream->WriteLine("<tr>");
   $cd = $rd->items[$y];
   for($a=0; $a < sizeof($nd->keys);$a ++)
   {
      $txtstream->WriteLine("<td style='color:navy;font-size:10px;font-
family:Cambria, serif;' align='left' nowrap><input Type= button value=\"\" . $cd-
>items[$a] . \"\"></input></td>");
   }
   $txtstream->WriteLine("</tr>");
}
```

Horizontal Using A ComboBox

```
for($y=0; $y < sizeof($rd->keys);$y ++)
```

```
{
    $txtstream->WriteLine("<tr>");
    $cd = $rd->items[$y];
    for($a=0; $a < sizeof($nd->keys);$a ++)
    {
        $txtstream->WriteLine("<td style='font-family:Calibri, Sans-Serif;font-size:
12px;color:navy;' align='left' nowrap='true'><select><option value = '"  . $cd-
>items[$a] . "'>" . $cd->items[$a] . "</option></select></td>\"  . vbcrlf)");
    }
    $txtstream->WriteLine("</tr>");
}
```

Horizontal Using A Div

```
for($y=0; $y < sizeof($rd->keys);$y ++)
{
    $txtstream->WriteLine("<tr>");
    $cd = $rd->items[$y];
    for($a=0; $a < sizeof($nd->keys);$a ++)
    {

        $txtstream->WriteLine("<td style='color:navy;font-size:10px;font-
family:Cambria, serif;' align='left' nowrap><div>" . $cd->items[$a] .
"</div></td>");

    }
    $txtstream->WriteLine("</tr>");
}
```

Horizontal Using A Link

```
for($y=0; $y < sizeof($rd->keys);$y ++)
{
    $txtstream->WriteLine("<tr>");
    $cd = $rd->items[$y];
```

```
    for($a=0; $a < sizeof($nd->keys);$a ++)
    {
  $txtstream->WriteLine("<td style='font-family:Calibri, Sans-Serif;font-size:
12px;color:navy;' align='left' nowrap='true'><a href='" . $cd->items[$a] . "'>" .
$cd->items[$a] . "</a></td>\" . vbcrlf)");
    }
    $txtstream->WriteLine("</tr>");
  }
```

Horizontal Using A ListBox

```
  for($y=0; $y < sizeof($rd->keys);$y ++)
  {
    $txtstream->WriteLine("Response.Write(\"<tr>\" & vbcrlf)");
    $cd = $rd->items[$y];
    for($a=0; $a < sizeof($nd->keys);$a ++)
    {
      $txtstream->WriteLine("<td style='font-family:Calibri, Sans-Serif;font-size:
12px;color:navy;' align='left' nowrap='true'><select multiple><option value = '" .
$cd->items[$a] . "'>" . $cd->items[$a] . "</option></select></td>\" . vbcrlf)");
    }
    $txtstream->WriteLine("</tr>");
  }
```

Horizontal Using A Span

```
  for($y=0; $y < sizeof($rd->keys);$y ++)
  {
    $txtstream->WriteLine("Response.Write(\"<tr>\" & vbcrlf)");
    $cd = $rd->items[$y];
    for($a=0; $a < sizeof($nd->keys);$a ++)
    {
      $txtstream->WriteLine("<td style='color:navy;font-size:10px;font-
family:Cambria, serif;' align='left' nowrap><span>" . $cd->items[$a] .
"</span></td>");
    }
    $txtstream->WriteLine("</tr>");
```

```
    }
```

Horizontal Using A Textarea

```
 for($y=0; $y < sizeof($rd->keys);$y ++)
   {
     $txtstream->WriteLine("Response.Write(\"<tr>\" & vbcrlf)");
     $cd = $rd->items[$y];
     for($a=0; $a < sizeof($nd->keys);$a ++)
     {
        $txtstream->WriteLine("<td style='color:navy;font-size:10px;font-
family:Cambria, serif;' align='left' nowrap><textarea>" . $cd->items[$a] .
"</textarea></td>");
     }
     $txtstream->WriteLine("</tr>");
   }
```

Horizontal Using A TextBox

```
   for($y=0; $y < sizeof($rd->keys);$y ++)
   {
     $txtstream->WriteLine("Response.Write(\"<tr>\" & vbcrlf)");
     $cd = $rd->items[$y];
     for($a=0; $a < sizeof($nd->keys);$a ++)
     {
        $txtstream->WriteLine("<td style='color:navy;font-size:10px;font-
family:Cambria, serif;' align='left' nowrap><input Type=text value=\"\" . $cd-
>items[$a] . \"\"></input></td>");


     }
     $txtstream->WriteLine("</tr>");
   }
```

Vertical No Additional Controls

```
for($a=0; $a < sizeof($nd->keys);$a ++)
{
    $txtstream->WriteLine("<tr><th style='color:darkred;font-size:10px;font-
family:Cambria, serif;' align='left' nowrap>" . $nd->items[$a]. "</th>");
    for($y=0; $y < sizeof($rd->keys);$y ++)
    {
        $cd = $rd->items[$y];
    $txtstream->WriteLine("<td style='color:navy;font-size:10px;font-
family:Cambria, serif;' align='left' nowrap>" . $cd->items[$a] . "</td>");
    }
    $txtstream->WriteLine("</tr>");
}
```

Vertical Using A Button

```
for($a=0; $a < sizeof($nd->keys);$a ++)
{
    $txtstream->WriteLine("<tr><th style='color:darkred;font-size:10px;font-
family:Cambria, serif;' align='left' nowrap>" . $nd->items[$a]. "</th>");
for($y=0; $y < sizeof($rd->keys);$y ++)
{
    $cd = $rd->items[$y];
    $txtstream->WriteLine("<td style='color:navy;font-size:10px;font-
family:Cambria, serif;' align='left' nowrap><input Type= button value=\"\" . $cd-
>items[$a] . \"\"></input></td>");
}
    $txtstream->WriteLine("</tr>");
}
```

Vertical Using A ComboBox

```
for($a=0; $a < sizeof($nd->keys);$a ++)
{
    $txtstream->WriteLine("<tr><th style='color:darkred;font-size:10px;font-
family:Cambria, serif;' align='left' nowrap>" . $nd->items[$a]. "</th>");
    for($y=0; $y < sizeof($rd->keys);$y ++)
```

```
    {
        $cd = $rd->items[$y];
$txtstream->WriteLine("<td style='font-family:Calibri, Sans-Serif;font-size:
12px;color:navy;' align='left' nowrap='true'><select><option value = '" . $cd-
>items[$a] . "'>" . $cd->items[$a] . "</option></select></td>\" . vbcrlf)");
    }
    $txtstream->WriteLine("</tr>");
}
```

Vertical Using A Div

```
for($a=0; $a < sizeof($nd->keys);$a ++)
{
    $txtstream->WriteLine("<tr><th style='color:darkred;font-size:10px;font-
family:Cambria, serif;' align='left' nowrap>" . $nd->items[$a]. "</th>");
    for($y=0; $y < sizeof($rd->keys);$y ++)
    {
        $cd = $rd->items[$y];
$txtstream->WriteLine("<td style='color:navy;font-size:10px;font-
family:Cambria, serif;' align='left' nowrap><div>" . $cd->items[$a] .
"</div></td>");
    }
    $txtstream->WriteLine("</tr>")
}
```

Vertical Using A Link

```
for($a=0; $a < sizeof($nd->keys);$a ++)
{
    $txtstream->WriteLine("<tr><th style='color:darkred;font-size:10px;font-
family:Cambria, serif;' align='left' nowrap>" . $nd->items[$a]. "</th>");
    for($y=0; $y < sizeof($rd->keys);$y ++)
    {
        $cd = $rd->items[$y];
$txtstream->WriteLine("<td style='font-family:Calibri, Sans-Serif;font-size:
12px;color:navy;' align='left' nowrap='true'><a href='" . $cd->items[$a] . "'>" .
$cd->items[$a] . "</a></td>\" . vbcrlf)");
```

```
    }
    $txtstream->WriteLine("</tr>");
  }
```

Vertical Using A ListBox

```
  for($a=0; $a < sizeof($nd->keys);$a ++)
  {
    $txtstream->WriteLine("<tr><th style='color:darkred;font-size:10px;font-
family:Cambria, serif;' align='left' nowrap>" . $nd->items[$a]. "</th>");
    for($y=0; $y < sizeof($rd->keys);$y ++)
    {
      $cd = $rd->items[$y];
      $txtstream->WriteLine("<td style='font-family:Calibri, Sans-Serif;font-size:
12px;color:navy;' align='left' nowrap='true'><select multiple><option value = '" .
$cd->items[$a]. "'>" . $cd->items[$a]. "</option></select></td>\" . vbcrlf)");
    }
    $txtstream->WriteLine("</tr>");
  }
```

Vertical Using A Span

```
  for($a=0; $a < sizeof($nd->keys);$a ++)
  {
    $txtstream->WriteLine("<tr><th style='color:darkred;font-size:10px;font-
family:Cambria, serif;' align='left' nowrap>" . $nd->items[$a]. "</th>");
    for($y=0; $y < sizeof($rd->keys);$y ++)
    {
      $cd = $rd->items[$y];
  $txtstream->WriteLine("<td style='color:navy;font-size:10px;font-
family:Cambria, serif;' align='left' nowrap><span>" . $cd->items[$a] .
"</span></td>");
    }
    $txtstream->WriteLine("</tr>");
  }
```

Vertical Using A Textarea

```
for($a=0; $a < sizeof($nd->keys);$a ++)
{
    $txtstream->WriteLine("<tr><th style='color:darkred;font-size:10px;font-
family:Cambria, serif;' align='left' nowrap>" . $nd->items[$a]. "</th>");
    for($y=0; $y < sizeof($rd->keys);$y ++)
    {
        $cd = $rd->items[$y];
  $txtstream->WriteLine("<td style='color:navy;font-size:10px;font-
family:Cambria, serif;' align='left' nowrap><textarea>" . $cd->items[$a] .
"</textarea></td>");
    }
    $txtstream->WriteLine("</tr>");
}
```

Vertical Using A TextBox

```
for($a=0; $a < sizeof($nd->keys);$a ++)
{
    $txtstream->WriteLine("<tr><th style='color:darkred;font-size:10px;font-
family:Cambria, serif;' align='left' nowrap>" . $nd->items[$a]. "</th>");
    for($y=0; $y < sizeof($rd->keys);$y ++)
    {
        $cd = $rd->items[$y];
  $txtstream->WriteLine("<td style='color:navy;font-size:10px;font-
family:Cambria, serif;' align='left' nowrap><input Type=text value=\"\" . $cd-
>items[$a] . \"\"></input></td>");
    }
    $txtstream->WriteLine("</tr>");
}
```

End Code

```
$txtstream->WriteLine("</table>");
$txtstream->WriteLine("</body>");
```

```
    $txtstream->WriteLine("</html>");
    $txtstream->Close();
}
```

Begin Code

```
function Write_The_Code()
{

   $ws = new COM("WScript.Shell");
   $filename = $ws->CurrentDirectory . "\\Win32_Process.hta";
   $fso = new COM("Scripting.FileSystemObject");
   var txtstream = $fso->OpenTextFile(filename, 2, true, -2);
   $txtstream->WriteLine("<html>");
   $txtstream->WriteLine("<head>");
   $txtstream->WriteLine("<title>Win32_Process</title>");
   $txtstream->WriteLine("</head>");
   $txtstream->WriteLine("<body>");
   $txtstream->WriteLine("<table  boder=0 cellpadding=2 cellspacing=2>");
```

Horizontal No Additional Tags

```
   for($y=0; $y < sizeof($rd->keys);$y ++)
   {
      $txtstream->WriteLine("<tr>");
```

```
    $cd = $rd->items[$y];
    for($a=0; $a < sizeof($nd->keys);$a ++)
    {
        $txtstream->WriteLine("<td style='color:navy;font-size:10px;font-
family:Cambria, serif;' align='left' nowrap>" . $cd->items[$a] . "</td>");
    }
    $txtstream->WriteLine("</tr>");
  }
```

Horizontal Using A Button

```
  for($y=0; $y < sizeof($rd->keys);$y ++)
  {
    $txtstream->WriteLine("<tr>");
    $cd = $rd->items[$y];
    for($a=0; $a < sizeof($nd->keys);$a ++)
    {
        $txtstream->WriteLine("<td style='color:navy;font-size:10px;font-
family:Cambria, serif;' align='left' nowrap><input Type= button value=\"\" . $cd-
>items[$a] . \"\"></input></td>");
    }
    $txtstream->WriteLine("</tr>");
  }
```

Horizontal Using A ComboBox

```
  for($y=0; $y < sizeof($rd->keys);$y ++)

  {

    $txtstream->WriteLine("<tr>");
    $cd = $rd->items[$y];
    for($a=0; $a < sizeof($nd->keys);$a ++)
    {
```

```
    $txtstream->WriteLine("<td style='font-family:Calibri, Sans-Serif;font-size:
12px;color:navy;' align='left' nowrap='true'><select><option value = '"  . $cd-
>items[$a] . "'>" . $cd->items[$a] . "</option></select></td>\" . vbcrlf)");
    }
    $txtstream->WriteLine("</tr>");
  }
```

Horizontal Using A Div

```
  for($y=0; $y < sizeof($rd->keys);$y ++)
  {
    $txtstream->WriteLine("<tr>");
    $cd = $rd->items[$y];
    for($a=0; $a < sizeof($nd->keys);$a ++)
    {

      $txtstream->WriteLine("<td style='color:navy;font-size:10px;font-
family:Cambria, serif;' align='left' nowrap><div>" . $cd->items[$a] .
"</div></td>");

    }
    $txtstream->WriteLine("</tr>");
  }
```

Horizontal Using A Link

```
  for($y=0; $y < sizeof($rd->keys);$y ++)
  {
    $txtstream->WriteLine("<tr>");
    $cd = $rd->items[$y];
    for($a=0; $a < sizeof($nd->keys);$a ++)
    {
  $txtstream->WriteLine("<td style='font-family:Calibri, Sans-Serif;font-size:
12px;color:navy;' align='left' nowrap='true'><a href='"  . $cd->items[$a] . "'>" .
$cd->items[$a] . "</a></td>\" . vbcrlf)");
```

```
    }
    $txtstream->WriteLine("</tr>");
}
```

Horizontal Using A ListBox

```
for($y=0; $y < sizeof($rd->keys);$y ++)
{
    $txtstream->WriteLine("Response.Write(\"<tr>\" & vbcrlf)");
    $cd = $rd->items[$y];
    for($a=0; $a < sizeof($nd->keys);$a ++)
    {
        $txtstream->WriteLine("<td style='font-family:Calibri, Sans-Serif;font-size:
12px;color:navy;' align='left' nowrap='true'><select multiple><option value = '" .
$cd->items[$a] . "'>" . $cd->items[$a] . "</option></select></td>\" . vbcrlf)");
    }
    $txtstream->WriteLine("</tr>");
}
```

Horizontal Using A Span

```
for($y=0; $y < sizeof($rd->keys);$y ++)
{
    $txtstream->WriteLine("Response.Write(\"<tr>\" & vbcrlf)");
    $cd = $rd->items[$y];
    for($a=0; $a < sizeof($nd->keys);$a ++)
    {
        $txtstream->WriteLine("<td style='color:navy;font-size:10px;font-
family:Cambria, serif;' align='left' nowrap><span>" . $cd->items[$a] .
"</span></td>");
    }
    $txtstream->WriteLine("</tr>");
}
```

Horizontal Using A Textarea

```
    for($y=0; $y < sizeof($rd->keys);$y ++)
    {
        $txtstream->WriteLine("Response.Write(\"<tr>\" & vbcrlf)");
        $cd = $rd->items[$y];
        for($a=0; $a < sizeof($nd->keys);$a ++)
        {
            $txtstream->WriteLine("<td style='color:navy;font-size:10px;font-
family:Cambria, serif;' align='left' nowrap><textarea>" . $cd->items[$a] .
"</textarea></td>");
        }
        $txtstream->WriteLine("</tr>");
    }
```

Horizontal Using A TextBox

```
    for($y=0; $y < sizeof($rd->keys);$y ++)
    {
        $txtstream->WriteLine("Response.Write(\"<tr>\" & vbcrlf)");
        $cd = $rd->items[$y];
        for($a=0; $a < sizeof($nd->keys);$a ++)
        {
            $txtstream->WriteLine("<td style='color:navy;font-size:10px;font-
family:Cambria, serif;' align='left' nowrap><input Type=text value=\"\" . $cd-
>items[$a] . \"\"></input></td>");

        }
        $txtstream->WriteLine("</tr>");
    }
```

Vertical No Additional Controls

```
    for($a=0; $a < sizeof($nd->keys);$a ++)
    {
        $txtstream->WriteLine("<tr><th style='color:darkred;font-size:10px;font-
family:Cambria, serif;' align='left' nowrap>" . $nd->items[$a]. "</th>");
        for($y=0; $y < sizeof($rd->keys);$y ++)
```

```
      {
        $cd = $rd->items[$y];
  $txtstream->WriteLine("<td style='color:navy;font-size:10px;font-
family:Cambria, serif;' align='left' nowrap>" . $cd->items[$a] . "</td>");
      }
      $txtstream->WriteLine("</tr>");
  }
```

Vertical Using A Button

```
  for($a=0; $a < sizeof($nd->keys);$a ++)
  {
      $txtstream->WriteLine("<tr><th style='color:darkred;font-size:10px;font-
family:Cambria, serif;' align='left' nowrap>" . $nd->items[$a]. "</th>");
  for($y=0; $y < sizeof($rd->keys);$y ++)
  {
    $cd = $rd->items[$y];
    $txtstream->WriteLine("<td style='color:navy;font-size:10px;font-
family:Cambria, serif;' align='left' nowrap><input Type= button value=\"\" . $cd-
>items[$a] . \"\"></input></td>");
  }
      $txtstream->WriteLine("</tr>");
  }
```

Vertical Using A ComboBox

```
  for($a=0; $a < sizeof($nd->keys);$a ++)
  {
      $txtstream->WriteLine("<tr><th style='color:darkred;font-size:10px;font-
family:Cambria, serif;' align='left' nowrap>" . $nd->items[$a]. "</th>");
      for($y=0; $y < sizeof($rd->keys);$y ++)
      {
        $cd = $rd->items[$y];
  $txtstream->WriteLine("<td style='font-family:Calibri, Sans-Serif;font-size:
12px;color:navy;' align='left' nowrap='true'><select><option value = '" . $cd-
>items[$a] . "'>" . $cd->items[$a] . "</option></select></td>\" . vbcrlf)");
```

```
        }
    $txtstream->WriteLine("</tr>");
  }
```

Vertical Using A Div

```
  for($a=0; $a < sizeof($nd->keys);$a ++)
  {
    $txtstream->WriteLine("<tr><th style='color:darkred;font-size:10px;font-
family:Cambria, serif;' align='left' nowrap>" . $nd->items[$a]. "</th>");
    for($y=0; $y < sizeof($rd->keys);$y ++)
    {
      $cd = $rd->items[$y];
  $txtstream->WriteLine("<td style='color:navy;font-size:10px;font-
family:Cambria, serif;' align='left' nowrap><div>" . $cd->items[$a] .
"</div></td>");
    }
    $txtstream->WriteLine("</tr>")
  }
```

Vertical Using A Link

```
  for($a=0; $a < sizeof($nd->keys);$a ++)
  {
    $txtstream->WriteLine("<tr><th style='color:darkred;font-size:10px;font-
family:Cambria, serif;' align='left' nowrap>" . $nd->items[$a]. "</th>");
    for($y=0; $y < sizeof($rd->keys);$y ++)
    {
      $cd = $rd->items[$y];
  $txtstream->WriteLine("<td style='font-family:Calibri, Sans-Serif;font-size:
12px;color:navy;' align='left' nowrap='true'><a href='" . $cd->items[$a] . "'>" .
$cd->items[$a] . "</a></td>\" . vbcrlf)");
    }
    $txtstream->WriteLine("</tr>");
  }
```

Vertical Using A ListBox

```
for($a=0; $a < sizeof($nd->keys);$a ++)
{
    $txtstream->WriteLine("<tr><th style='color:darkred;font-size:10px;font-
family:Cambria, serif;' align='left' nowrap>" . $nd->items[$a]. "</th>");
    for($y=0; $y < sizeof($rd->keys);$y ++)
    {
        $cd = $rd->items[$y];
        $txtstream->WriteLine("<td style='font-family:Calibri, Sans-Serif;font-size:
12px;color:navy;' align='left' nowrap='true'><select multiple><option value = '" .
$cd->items[$a] . "'>" . $cd->items[$a] . "</option></select></td>\" . vbcrlf)");
    }
    $txtstream->WriteLine("</tr>");
}
```

Vertical Using A Span

```
for($a=0; $a < sizeof($nd->keys);$a ++)
{
    $txtstream->WriteLine("<tr><th style='color:darkred;font-size:10px;font-
family:Cambria, serif;' align='left' nowrap>" . $nd->items[$a]. "</th>");
    for($y=0; $y < sizeof($rd->keys);$y ++)
    {
        $cd = $rd->items[$y];
    $txtstream->WriteLine("<td style='color:navy;font-size:10px;font-
family:Cambria, serif;' align='left' nowrap><span>" . $cd->items[$a] .
"</span></td>");
    }
    $txtstream->WriteLine("</tr>");
}
```

Vertical Using A Textarea

```
for($a=0; $a < sizeof($nd->keys);$a ++)
{
    $txtstream->WriteLine("<tr><th style='color:darkred;font-size:10px;font-
family:Cambria, serif;' align='left' nowrap>" . $nd->items[$a]. "</th>");
```

```
    for($y=0; $y < sizeof($rd->keys);$y ++)
    {
        $cd = $rd->items[$y];
$txtstream->WriteLine("<td style='color:navy;font-size:10px;font-
family:Cambria, serif;' align='left' nowrap><textarea>" . $cd->items[$a] .
"</textarea></td>");
    }
    $txtstream->WriteLine("</tr>");
  }
```

Vertical Using A TextBox

```
    for($a=0; $a < sizeof($nd->keys);$a ++)
    {
        $txtstream->WriteLine("<tr><th style='color:darkred;font-size:10px;font-
family:Cambria, serif;' align='left' nowrap>" . $nd->items[$a]. "</th>");
        for($y=0; $y < sizeof($rd->keys);$y ++)
        {
            $cd = $rd->items[$y];
$txtstream->WriteLine("<td style='color:navy;font-size:10px;font-
family:Cambria, serif;' align='left' nowrap><input Type=text value=\"\" . $cd-
>items[$a] . \"\"></input></td>");
        }
        $txtstream->WriteLine("</tr>");
    }
```

End Code

```
    $txtstream->WriteLine("</table>");
    $txtstream->WriteLine("</body>");
    $txtstream->WriteLine("</html>");
    $txtstream->Close();
}
```

HTML TABLES

Begin Code

```
function Write_The_Code()
{

    $ws = new COM("WScript.Shell");
    $filename = $ws->CurrentDirectory . "\\Win32_Process.hta";
    $fso = new COM("Scripting.FileSystemObject");
    var txtstream = $fso->OpenTextFile(filename, 2, true, -2);
    $txtstream->WriteLine("<html>");
    $txtstream->WriteLine("<head>");
    $txtstream->WriteLine("<title>Win32_Process</title>");
    $txtstream->WriteLine("</head>");
    $txtstream->WriteLine("<body>");
    $txtstream->WriteLine("<table  boder=1 cellpadding=2 cellspacing=2>");
```

Horizontal No Additional Tags

```
    for($y=0; $y < sizeof($rd->keys);$y ++)
    {
        $txtstream->WriteLine("<tr>");
        $cd = $rd->items[$y];
        for($a=0; $a < sizeof($nd->keys);$a ++)
```

```
     {
         $txtstream->WriteLine("<td style='color:navy;font-size:10px;font-
family:Cambria, serif;' align='left' nowrap>" . $cd->items[$a] . "</td>");
     }
     $txtstream->WriteLine("</tr>");
  }
```

Horizontal Using A Button

```
  for($y=0; $y < sizeof($rd->keys);$y ++)
  {
     $txtstream->WriteLine("<tr>");
     $cd = $rd->items[$y];
     for($a=0; $a < sizeof($nd->keys);$a ++)
     {
         $txtstream->WriteLine("<td style='color:navy;font-size:10px;font-
family:Cambria, serif;' align='left' nowrap><input Type= button value=\"\" . $cd-
>items[$a] . \"\"></input></td>");
     }
     $txtstream->WriteLine("</tr>");
  }
```

Horizontal Using A ComboBox

```
  for($y=0; $y < sizeof($rd->keys);$y ++)

  {

     $txtstream->WriteLine("<tr>");
     $cd = $rd->items[$y];
     for($a=0; $a < sizeof($nd->keys);$a ++)
     {
         $txtstream->WriteLine("<td style='font-family:Calibri, Sans-Serif;font-size:
12px;color:navy;' align='left' nowrap='true'><select><option value = '" . $cd-
>items[$a] . "'>" . $cd->items[$a] . "</option></select></td>\" . vbcrlf)");
```

```
    }
    $txtstream->WriteLine("</tr>");
  }
```

Horizontal Using A Div

```
  for($y=0; $y < sizeof($rd->keys);$y ++)
  {
    $txtstream->WriteLine("<tr>");
    $cd = $rd->items[$y];
    for($a=0; $a < sizeof($nd->keys);$a ++)
    {

      $txtstream->WriteLine("<td style='color:navy;font-size:10px;font-
family:Cambria, serif;' align='left' nowrap><div>" . $cd->items[$a] .
"</div></td>");

    }
    $txtstream->WriteLine("</tr>");
  }
```

Horizontal Using A Link

```
  for($y=0; $y < sizeof($rd->keys);$y ++)
  {
    $txtstream->WriteLine("<tr>");
    $cd = $rd->items[$y];
    for($a=0; $a < sizeof($nd->keys);$a ++)
    {
  $txtstream->WriteLine("<td style='font-family:Calibri, Sans-Serif;font-size:
12px;color:navy;' align='left' nowrap='true'><a href='" . $cd->items[$a] . "'>" .
$cd->items[$a] . "</a></td>\" . vbcrlf)");
    }
    $txtstream->WriteLine("</tr>");
  }
```

Horizontal Using A ListBox

```
for($y=0; $y < sizeof($rd->keys);$y ++)
{
   $txtstream->WriteLine("Response.Write(\"<tr>\" & vbcrlf)");
   $cd = $rd->items[$y];
   for($a=0; $a < sizeof($nd->keys);$a ++)
   {
      $txtstream->WriteLine("<td style='font-family:Calibri, Sans-Serif;font-size:
12px;color:navy;' align='left' nowrap='true'><select multiple><option value = '" .
$cd->items[$a] . "'>" . $cd->items[$a] . "</option></select></td>\" . vbcrlf)");
   }
   $txtstream->WriteLine("</tr>");
}
```

Horizontal Using A Span

```
for($y=0; $y < sizeof($rd->keys);$y ++)
{
   $txtstream->WriteLine("Response.Write(\"<tr>\" & vbcrlf)");
   $cd = $rd->items[$y];
   for($a=0; $a < sizeof($nd->keys);$a ++)
   {
      $txtstream->WriteLine("<td style='color:navy;font-size:10px;font-
family:Cambria, serif;' align='left' nowrap><span>" . $cd->items[$a] .
"</span></td>");
   }
   $txtstream->WriteLine("</tr>");
}
```

Horizontal Using A Textarea

```
for($y=0; $y < sizeof($rd->keys);$y ++)
{
   $txtstream->WriteLine("Response.Write(\"<tr>\" & vbcrlf)");
```

```
    $cd = $rd->items[$y];
    for($a=0; $a < sizeof($nd->keys);$a ++)
    {
        $txtstream->WriteLine("<td style='color:navy;font-size:10px;font-
family:Cambria, serif;' align='left' nowrap><textarea>" . $cd->items[$a] .
"</textarea></td>");
    }
    $txtstream->WriteLine("</tr>");
}
```

Horizontal Using A TextBox

```
for($y=0; $y < sizeof($rd->keys);$y ++)
{
    $txtstream->WriteLine("Response.Write(\"<tr>\" & vbcrlf)");
    $cd = $rd->items[$y];
    for($a=0; $a < sizeof($nd->keys);$a ++)
    {
        $txtstream->WriteLine("<td style='color:navy;font-size:10px;font-
family:Cambria, serif;' align='left' nowrap><input Type=text value=\"\" . $cd-
>items[$a] . \"\"></input></td>");

    }
    $txtstream->WriteLine("</tr>");
}
```

Vertical No Additional Controls

```
for($a=0; $a < sizeof($nd->keys);$a ++)
{
    $txtstream->WriteLine("<tr><th style='color:darkred;font-size:10px;font-
family:Cambria, serif;' align='left' nowrap>" . $nd->items[$a]. "</th>");
    for($y=0; $y < sizeof($rd->keys);$y ++)
    {
        $cd = $rd->items[$y];
```

```
    $txtstream->WriteLine("<td style='color:navy;font-size:10px;font-
family:Cambria, serif;' align='left' nowrap>" . $cd->items[$a] . "</td>");
        }
    $txtstream->WriteLine("</tr>");
  }
```

Vertical Using A Button

```
  for($a=0; $a < sizeof($nd->keys);$a ++)
  {
    $txtstream->WriteLine("<tr><th style='color:darkred;font-size:10px;font-
family:Cambria, serif;' align='left' nowrap>" . $nd->items[$a]. "</th>");
for($y=0; $y < sizeof($rd->keys);$y ++)
{
  $cd = $rd->items[$y];
  $txtstream->WriteLine("<td style='color:navy;font-size:10px;font-
family:Cambria, serif;' align='left' nowrap><input Type= button value=\"\" . $cd-
>items[$a] . \"\"></input></td>");
}
    $txtstream->WriteLine("</tr>");
   }
```

Vertical Using A ComboBox

```
  for($a=0; $a < sizeof($nd->keys);$a ++)
  {
    $txtstream->WriteLine("<tr><th style='color:darkred;font-size:10px;font-
family:Cambria, serif;' align='left' nowrap>" . $nd->items[$a]. "</th>");
    for($y=0; $y < sizeof($rd->keys);$y ++)
    {
      $cd = $rd->items[$y];
  $txtstream->WriteLine("<td style='font-family:Calibri, Sans-Serif;font-size:
12px;color:navy;' align='left' nowrap='true'><select><option value = '" . $cd-
>items[$a] . "'>" . $cd->items[$a] . "</option></select></td>\" . vbcrlf)");
      }
    $txtstream->WriteLine("</tr>");
```

```
}
```

Vertical Using A Div

```
for($a=0; $a < sizeof($nd->keys);$a ++)
{
    $txtstream->WriteLine("<tr><th style='color:darkred;font-size:10px;font-
family:Cambria, serif;' align='left' nowrap>" . $nd->items[$a]. "</th>");
    for($y=0; $y < sizeof($rd->keys);$y ++)
    {
        $cd = $rd->items[$y];
  $txtstream->WriteLine("<td style='color:navy;font-size:10px;font-
family.Cambria, serif;' align='left' nowrap><div>" . $cd->items[$a] .
"</div></td>");
    }
    $txtstream->WriteLine("</tr>")
}
```

Vertical Using A Link

```
for($a=0; $a < sizeof($nd->keys);$a ++)
{
    $txtstream->WriteLine("<tr><th style='color:darkred;font-size:10px;font-
family:Cambria, serif;' align='left' nowrap>" . $nd->items[$a]. "</th>");
    for($y=0; $y < sizeof($rd->keys);$y ++)
    {
        $cd = $rd->items[$y];
  $txtstream->WriteLine("<td style='font-family:Calibri, Sans-Serif;font-size:
12px;color:navy;' align='left' nowrap='true'><a href='" . $cd->items[$a] . "'>" .
$cd->items[$a] . "</a></td>\" . vbcrlf)");
    }
    $txtstream->WriteLine("</tr>");
}
```

Vertical Using A ListBox

```
for($a=0; $a < sizeof($nd->keys);$a ++)
{
    $txtstream->WriteLine("<tr><th style='color:darkred;font-size:10px;font-
family:Cambria, serif;' align='left' nowrap>" . $nd->items[$a]. "</th>");
    for($y=0; $y < sizeof($rd->keys);$y ++)
    {
       $cd = $rd->items[$y];
       $txtstream->WriteLine("<td style='font-family:Calibri, Sans-Serif;font-size:
12px;color:navy;' align='left' nowrap='true'><select multiple><option value = '" .
$cd->items[$a] . "'>" . $cd->items[$a] . "</option></select></td>\" . vbcrlf)");
    }
    $txtstream->WriteLine("</tr>");
}
```

Vertical Using A Span

```
for($a=0; $a < sizeof($nd->keys);$a ++)
{
    $txtstream->WriteLine("<tr><th style='color:darkred;font-size:10px;font-
family:Cambria, serif;' align='left' nowrap>" . $nd->items[$a]. "</th>");
    for($y=0; $y < sizeof($rd->keys);$y ++)
    {
       $cd = $rd->items[$y];
  $txtstream->WriteLine("<td style='color:navy;font-size:10px;font-
family:Cambria, serif;' align='left' nowrap><span>" . $cd->items[$a] .
"</span></td>");
    }
    $txtstream->WriteLine("</tr>");
}
```

Vertical Using A Textarea

```
for($a=0; $a < sizeof($nd->keys);$a ++)
{
    $txtstream->WriteLine("<tr><th style='color:darkred;font-size:10px;font-
family:Cambria, serif;' align='left' nowrap>" . $nd->items[$a]. "</th>");
```

```
     for($y=0; $y < sizeof($rd->keys);$y ++)
     {
         $cd = $rd->items[$y];
   $txtstream->WriteLine("<td style='color:navy;font-size:10px;font-
family:Cambria, serif;' align='left' nowrap><textarea>" . $cd->items[$a] .
"</textarea></td>");
     }
     $txtstream->WriteLine("</tr>");
  }
```

Vertical Using A TextBox

```
  for($a=0; $a < sizeof($nd->keys);$a ++)
  {
     $txtstream->WriteLine("<tr><th style='color:darkred;font-size:10px;font-
family:Cambria, serif;' align='left' nowrap>" . $nd->items[$a]. "</th>");
     for($y=0; $y < sizeof($rd->keys);$y ++)
     {
         $cd = $rd->items[$y];
   $txtstream->WriteLine("<td style='color:navy;font-size:10px;font-
family:Cambria, serif;' align='left' nowrap><input Type=text value=\"\" . $cd-
>items[$a] . \"\"></input></td>");
     }
     $txtstream->WriteLine("</tr>");
  }
```

End Code

```
  $txtstream->WriteLine("</table>");
  $txtstream->WriteLine("</body>");
  $txtstream->WriteLine("</html>");
  $txtstream->Close();
}
```

Stylesheets

Decorating your web pages

BELOW ARE SOME STYLESHEETS I COOKED UP THAT I LIKE AND THINK YOU MIGHT TOO. Don't worry I won't be offended if you take and modify to your hearts delight. Please do!

NONE

```
$txtstream->WriteLine('<style type='text/css'>")
$txtstream->WriteLine("   th")
$txtstream->WriteLine("   }")
$txtstream->WriteLine("   COLOR: darkred;")
$txtstream->WriteLine("   BACKGROUND-COLOR: white;")
$txtstream->WriteLine("   FONT-FAMILY:font-family: Cambria, serif;")
$txtstream->WriteLine("   FONT-SIZE: 12px;")
$txtstream->WriteLine("   text-align: left;")
$txtstream->WriteLine("   white-Space: nowrap;")
$txtstream->WriteLine("   }")
```

```
$txtstream->WriteLine("    td")
$txtstream->WriteLine("    }")
$txtstream->WriteLine("    COLOR: navy;")
$txtstream->WriteLine("    BACKGROUND-COLOR: white;")
$txtstream->WriteLine("    FONT-FAMILY: font-family: Cambria, serif;")
$txtstream->WriteLine("    FONT-SIZE: 12px;")
$txtstream->WriteLine("    text-align: left;")
$txtstream->WriteLine("    white-Space: nowrap;")
$txtstream->WriteLine("    }")
$txtstream->WriteLine("    </style>');
```

BLACK AND WHITE TEXT

```
$txtstream->WriteLine("    <style type='text/css'>');
$txtstream->WriteLine("    th")
$txtstream->WriteLine("    }")
$txtstream->WriteLine("      COLOR: white;")
$txtstream->WriteLine("      BACKGROUND-COLOR: black;")
$txtstream->WriteLine("      FONT-FAMILY:font-family: Cambria, serif;")
$txtstream->WriteLine("      FONT-SIZE: 12px;")
$txtstream->WriteLine("      text-align: left;")
$txtstream->WriteLine("      white-Space: nowrap;")
$txtstream->WriteLine("    }")
$txtstream->WriteLine("    td")
$txtstream->WriteLine("    }")
$txtstream->WriteLine("      COLOR: white;")
$txtstream->WriteLine("      BACKGROUND-COLOR: black;")
$txtstream->WriteLine("      FONT-FAMILY: font-family: Cambria, serif;")
$txtstream->WriteLine("      FONT-SIZE: 12px;")
$txtstream->WriteLine("      text-align: left;")
$txtstream->WriteLine("      white-Space: nowrap;")
$txtstream->WriteLine("    }")
```

```
$txtstream->WriteLine("    div")
$txtstream->WriteLine("    }")
$txtstream->WriteLine("      COLOR: white;")
$txtstream->WriteLine("      BACKGROUND-COLOR: black;")
$txtstream->WriteLine("      FONT-FAMILY: font-family: Cambria, serif;")
$txtstream->WriteLine("      FONT-SIZE: 10px;")
$txtstream->WriteLine("      text-align: left;")
$txtstream->WriteLine("      white-Space: nowrap;")
$txtstream->WriteLine("    }")
$txtstream->WriteLine("    span")
$txtstream->WriteLine("    }")
$txtstream->WriteLine("      COLOR: white;")
$txtstream->WriteLine("      BACKGROUND-COLOR: black;")
$txtstream->WriteLine("      FONT-FAMILY: font-family: Cambria, serif;")
$txtstream->WriteLine("      FONT-SIZE: 10px;")
$txtstream->WriteLine("      text-align: left;")
$txtstream->WriteLine("      white-Space: nowrap;")
$txtstream->WriteLine("      display:inline-block;")
$txtstream->WriteLine("      width: 100%;")
$txtstream->WriteLine("    }")
$txtstream->WriteLine("    textarea")
$txtstream->WriteLine("    }")
$txtstream->WriteLine("      COLOR: white;")
$txtstream->WriteLine("      BACKGROUND-COLOR: black;")
$txtstream->WriteLine("      FONT-FAMILY: font-family: Cambria, serif;")
$txtstream->WriteLine("      FONT-SIZE: 10px;")
$txtstream->WriteLine("      text-align: left;")
$txtstream->WriteLine("      white-Space: nowrap;")
$txtstream->WriteLine("      width: 100%;")
$txtstream->WriteLine("    }")
$txtstream->WriteLine("    select")
$txtstream->WriteLine("    }")
$txtstream->WriteLine("      COLOR: white;")
```

```
$txtstream->WriteLine("        BACKGROUND-COLOR: black;")
$txtstream->WriteLine("        FONT-FAMILY: font-family: Cambria, serif;")
$txtstream->WriteLine("        FONT-SIZE: 10px;")
$txtstream->WriteLine("        text-align: left;")
$txtstream->WriteLine("        white-Space: nowrap;")
$txtstream->WriteLine("        width: 100%;")
$txtstream->WriteLine("    }")
$txtstream->WriteLine("    input")
$txtstream->WriteLine("    }")
$txtstream->WriteLine("        COLOR: white;")
$txtstream->WriteLine("        BACKGROUND-COLOR: black;")
$txtstream->WriteLine("        FONT-FAMILY: font-family: Cambria, serif;")
$txtstream->WriteLine("        FONT-SIZE: 12px;")
$txtstream->WriteLine("        text-align: left;")
$txtstream->WriteLine("        display:table-cell;")
$txtstream->WriteLine("        white-Space: nowrap;")
$txtstream->WriteLine("    }")
$txtstream->WriteLine("    h1 }")
$txtstream->WriteLine("    color: antiquewhite;")
$txtstream->WriteLine("    text-shadow: 1px 1px 1px black;")
$txtstream->WriteLine("    padding: 3px;")
$txtstream->WriteLine("    text-align: center;")
$txtstream->WriteLine("     box-shadow: inset 2px 2px 5px rgba(0,0,0,0.5);;, inset -2px -2px 5px rgba(255,255,255,0.5);;")
$txtstream->WriteLine("    }")
$txtstream->WriteLine("    </style>');
```

COLORED TEXT

```
$txtstream->WriteLine("    <style type='text/css'>');
$txtstream->WriteLine("    th")
$txtstream->WriteLine("    }")
$txtstream->WriteLine("        COLOR: darkred;")
```

```
$txtstream->WriteLine("      BACKGROUND-COLOR: #eeeeee;")
$txtstream->WriteLine("      FONT-FAMILY:font-family: Cambria, serif;")
$txtstream->WriteLine("      FONT-SIZE: 12px;")
$txtstream->WriteLine("      text-align: left;")
$txtstream->WriteLine("      white-Space: nowrap;")
$txtstream->WriteLine("   }")
$txtstream->WriteLine("   td")
$txtstream->WriteLine("   }")
$txtstream->WriteLine("      COLOR: navy;")
$txtstream->WriteLine("      BACKGROUND-COLOR: #eeeeee;")
$txtstream->WriteLine("      FONT-FAMILY: font-family: Cambria, serif;")
$txtstream->WriteLine("      FONT-SIZE: 12px;")
$txtstream->WriteLine("      text-align: left;")
$txtstream->WriteLine("      white-Space: nowrap;")
$txtstream->WriteLine("   }")
$txtstream->WriteLine("   div")
$txtstream->WriteLine("   }")
$txtstream->WriteLine("      COLOR: white;")
$txtstream->WriteLine("      BACKGROUND-COLOR: navy;")
$txtstream->WriteLine("      FONT-FAMILY: font-family: Cambria, serif;")
$txtstream->WriteLine("      FONT-SIZE: 10px;")
$txtstream->WriteLine("      text-align: left;")
$txtstream->WriteLine("      white-Space: nowrap;")
$txtstream->WriteLine("   }")
$txtstream->WriteLine("   span")
$txtstream->WriteLine("   }")
$txtstream->WriteLine("      COLOR: white;")
$txtstream->WriteLine("      BACKGROUND-COLOR: navy;")
$txtstream->WriteLine("      FONT-FAMILY: font-family: Cambria, serif;")
$txtstream->WriteLine("      FONT-SIZE: 10px;")
$txtstream->WriteLine("      text-align: left;")
$txtstream->WriteLine("      white-Space: nowrap;")
$txtstream->WriteLine("      display:inline-block;")
```

```
$txtstream->WriteLine("    width: 100%;")
$txtstream->WriteLine("  }")
$txtstream->WriteLine("  textarea")
$txtstream->WriteLine("  }")
$txtstream->WriteLine("    COLOR: white;")
$txtstream->WriteLine("    BACKGROUND-COLOR: navy;")
$txtstream->WriteLine("    FONT-FAMILY: font-family: Cambria, serif;")
$txtstream->WriteLine("    FONT-SIZE: 10px;")
$txtstream->WriteLine("    text-align: left;")
$txtstream->WriteLine("    white-Space: nowrap;")
$txtstream->WriteLine("    width: 100%;")
$txtstream->WriteLine("  }")
$txtstream->WriteLine("  select")
$txtstream->WriteLine("  }")
$txtstream->WriteLine("    COLOR: white;")
$txtstream->WriteLine("    BACKGROUND-COLOR: navy;")
$txtstream->WriteLine("    FONT-FAMILY: font-family: Cambria, serif;")
$txtstream->WriteLine("    FONT-SIZE: 10px;")
$txtstream->WriteLine("    text-align: left;")
$txtstream->WriteLine("    white-Space: nowrap;")
$txtstream->WriteLine("    width: 100%;")
$txtstream->WriteLine("  }")
$txtstream->WriteLine("  input")
$txtstream->WriteLine("  }")
$txtstream->WriteLine("    COLOR: white;")
$txtstream->WriteLine("    BACKGROUND-COLOR: navy;")
$txtstream->WriteLine("    FONT-FAMILY: font-family: Cambria, serif;")
$txtstream->WriteLine("    FONT-SIZE: 12px;")
$txtstream->WriteLine("    text-align: left;")
$txtstream->WriteLine("    display:table-cell;")
$txtstream->WriteLine("    white-Space: nowrap;")
$txtstream->WriteLine("  }")
$txtstream->WriteLine("  h1 }")
```

```
$txtstream->WriteLine("    color: antiquewhite;")
$txtstream->WriteLine("    text-shadow: 1px 1px 1px black;")
$txtstream->WriteLine("    padding: 3px;")
$txtstream->WriteLine("    text-align: center;")
$txtstream->WriteLine("      box-shadow: inset 2px 2px 5px rgba(0,0,0,0.5);,
inset -2px -2px 5px rgba(255,255,255,0.5);;")
$txtstream->WriteLine("    }")
$txtstream->WriteLine("    </style>');
```

OSCILLATING ROW COLORS

```
$txtstream->WriteLine("    <style>');
$txtstream->WriteLine("    th")
$txtstream->WriteLine("    }")
$txtstream->WriteLine("      COLOR: white;")
$txtstream->WriteLine("      BACKGROUND-COLOR: navy;")
$txtstream->WriteLine("      FONT-FAMILY:font-family: Cambria, serif;")
$txtstream->WriteLine("      FONT-SIZE: 12px;")
$txtstream->WriteLine("      text-align: left;")
$txtstream->WriteLine("      white-Space: nowrap;")
$txtstream->WriteLine("    }")
$txtstream->WriteLine("    td")
$txtstream->WriteLine("    }")
$txtstream->WriteLine("      COLOR: navy;")
$txtstream->WriteLine("      FONT-FAMILY: font-family: Cambria, serif;")
$txtstream->WriteLine("      FONT-SIZE: 12px;")
$txtstream->WriteLine("      text-align: left;")
$txtstream->WriteLine("      white-Space: nowrap;")
$txtstream->WriteLine("    }")
$txtstream->WriteLine("    div")
$txtstream->WriteLine("    }")
```

```
$txtstream->WriteLine("        COLOR: navy;")
$txtstream->WriteLine("        FONT-FAMILY: font-family: Cambria, serif;")
$txtstream->WriteLine("        FONT-SIZE: 12px;")
$txtstream->WriteLine("        text-align: left;")
$txtstream->WriteLine("        white-Space: nowrap;")
$txtstream->WriteLine("    }")
$txtstream->WriteLine("    span")
$txtstream->WriteLine("    }")
$txtstream->WriteLine("        COLOR: navy;")
$txtstream->WriteLine("        FONT-FAMILY: font-family: Cambria, serif;")
$txtstream->WriteLine("        FONT-SIZE: 12px;")
$txtstream->WriteLine("        text-align: left;")
$txtstream->WriteLine("        white-Space: nowrap;")
$txtstream->WriteLine("        width: 100%;")
$txtstream->WriteLine("    }")
$txtstream->WriteLine("    textarea")
$txtstream->WriteLine("    }")
$txtstream->WriteLine("        COLOR: navy;")
$txtstream->WriteLine("        FONT-FAMILY: font-family: Cambria, serif;")
$txtstream->WriteLine("        FONT-SIZE: 12px;")
$txtstream->WriteLine("        text-align: left;")
$txtstream->WriteLine("        white-Space: nowrap;")
$txtstream->WriteLine("        display:inline-block;")
$txtstream->WriteLine("        width: 100%;")
$txtstream->WriteLine("    }")
$txtstream->WriteLine("    select")
$txtstream->WriteLine("    }")
$txtstream->WriteLine("        COLOR: navy;")
$txtstream->WriteLine("        FONT-FAMILY: font-family: Cambria, serif;")
$txtstream->WriteLine("        FONT-SIZE: 10px;")
$txtstream->WriteLine("        text-align: left;")
$txtstream->WriteLine("        white-Space: nowrap;")
$txtstream->WriteLine("        display:inline-block;")
```

```
$txtstream->WriteLine("    width: 100%;")
$txtstream->WriteLine("  }")
$txtstream->WriteLine("  input")
$txtstream->WriteLine("  }")
$txtstream->WriteLine("    COLOR: navy;")
$txtstream->WriteLine("    FONT-FAMILY: font-family: Cambria, serif;")
$txtstream->WriteLine("    FONT-SIZE: 12px;")
$txtstream->WriteLine("    text-align: left;")
$txtstream->WriteLine("    display:table-cell;")
$txtstream->WriteLine("    white-Space: nowrap;")
$txtstream->WriteLine("  }")
$txtstream->WriteLine("  h1 }")
$txtstream->WriteLine("  color: antiquewhite;")
$txtstream->WriteLine("  text-shadow: 1px 1px 1px black;")
$txtstream->WriteLine("  padding: 3px;")
$txtstream->WriteLine("  text-align: center;")
$txtstream->WriteLine("    box-shadow: inset 2px 2px 5px rgba(0,0,0,0.5);,
inset -2px -2px 5px rgba(255,255,255,0.5);;")
$txtstream->WriteLine("  }")
$txtstream->WriteLine("  tr:nth-child(even);}background-color:#f2f2f2;}")
$txtstream->WriteLine("        tr:nth-child(odd);}background-color:#cccccc;
color:#f2f2f2;}")
$txtstream->WriteLine("  </style>');
```

GHOST DECORATED

```
$txtstream->WriteLine("  <style type='text/css'>');
$txtstream->WriteLine("  th")
$txtstream->WriteLine("  }")
$txtstream->WriteLine("    COLOR: black;")
$txtstream->WriteLine("    BACKGROUND-COLOR: white;")
$txtstream->WriteLine("    FONT-FAMILY:font-family: Cambria, serif;")
$txtstream->WriteLine("    FONT-SIZE: 12px;")
```

```
$txtstream->WriteLine("      text-align: left;")
$txtstream->WriteLine("      white-Space: nowrap;")
$txtstream->WriteLine("    }")
$txtstream->WriteLine("   td")
$txtstream->WriteLine("    }")
$txtstream->WriteLine("      COLOR: black;")
$txtstream->WriteLine("      BACKGROUND-COLOR: white;")
$txtstream->WriteLine("      FONT-FAMILY: font-family: Cambria, serif;")
$txtstream->WriteLine("      FONT-SIZE: 12px;")
$txtstream->WriteLine("      text-align: left;")
$txtstream->WriteLine("      white-Space: nowrap;")
$txtstream->WriteLine("    }")
$txtstream->WriteLine("   div")
$txtstream->WriteLine("    }")
$txtstream->WriteLine("      COLOR: black;")
$txtstream->WriteLine("      BACKGROUND-COLOR: white;")
$txtstream->WriteLine("      FONT-FAMILY: font-family: Cambria, serif;")
$txtstream->WriteLine("      FONT-SIZE: 10px;")
$txtstream->WriteLine("      text-align: left;")
$txtstream->WriteLine("      white-Space: nowrap;")
$txtstream->WriteLine("    }")
$txtstream->WriteLine("   span")
$txtstream->WriteLine("    }")
$txtstream->WriteLine("      COLOR: black;")
$txtstream->WriteLine("      BACKGROUND-COLOR: white;")
$txtstream->WriteLine("      FONT-FAMILY: font-family: Cambria, serif;")
$txtstream->WriteLine("      FONT-SIZE: 10px;")
$txtstream->WriteLine("      text-align: left;")
$txtstream->WriteLine("      white-Space: nowrap;")
$txtstream->WriteLine("      display:inline-block;")
$txtstream->WriteLine("      width: 100%;")
$txtstream->WriteLine("    }")
$txtstream->WriteLine("   textarea")
```

```
$txtstream->WriteLine("    }")
$txtstream->WriteLine("      COLOR: black;")
$txtstream->WriteLine("      BACKGROUND-COLOR: white;")
$txtstream->WriteLine("      FONT-FAMILY: font-family: Cambria, serif;")
$txtstream->WriteLine("      FONT-SIZE: 10px;")
$txtstream->WriteLine("      text-align: left;")
$txtstream->WriteLine("      white-Space: nowrap;")
$txtstream->WriteLine("      width: 100%;")
$txtstream->WriteLine("    }")
$txtstream->WriteLine("   select")
$txtstream->WriteLine("    }")
$txtstream->WriteLine("      COLOR: black;")
$txtstream->WriteLine("      BACKGROUND-COLOR: white;")
$txtstream->WriteLine("      FONT-FAMILY: font-family: Cambria, serif;")
$txtstream->WriteLine("      FONT-SIZE: 10px;")
$txtstream->WriteLine("      text-align: left;")
$txtstream->WriteLine("      white-Space: nowrap;")
$txtstream->WriteLine("      width: 100%;")
$txtstream->WriteLine("    }")
$txtstream->WriteLine("   input")
$txtstream->WriteLine("    }")
$txtstream->WriteLine("      COLOR: black;")
$txtstream->WriteLine("      BACKGROUND-COLOR: white;")
$txtstream->WriteLine("      FONT-FAMILY: font-family: Cambria, serif;")
$txtstream->WriteLine("      FONT-SIZE: 12px;")
$txtstream->WriteLine("      text-align: left;")
$txtstream->WriteLine("      display:table-cell;")
$txtstream->WriteLine("      white-Space: nowrap;")
$txtstream->WriteLine("    }")
$txtstream->WriteLine("   h1 }")
$txtstream->WriteLine("   color: antiquewhite;")
$txtstream->WriteLine("   text-shadow: 1px 1px 1px black;")
$txtstream->WriteLine("   padding: 3px;")
```

```
$txtstream->WriteLine("    text-align: center;")
$txtstream->WriteLine("     box-shadow: inset 2px 2px 5px rgba(0,0,0,0.5);,
inset -2px -2px 5px rgba(255,255,255,0.5);;")
$txtstream->WriteLine("   }")
$txtstream->WriteLine("   </style>');
```

3D

```
$txtstream->WriteLine("   <style type='text/css'>');
$txtstream->WriteLine("   body")
$txtstream->WriteLine("   }")
$txtstream->WriteLine("      PADDING-RIGHT: 0px;")
$txtstream->WriteLine("      PADDING-LEFT: 0px;")
$txtstream->WriteLine("      PADDING-BOTTOM: 0px;")
$txtstream->WriteLine("      MARGIN: 0px;")
$txtstream->WriteLine("      COLOR: #333;")
$txtstream->WriteLine("      PADDING-TOP: 0px;")
$txtstream->WriteLine("        FONT-FAMILY: verdana, arial, helvetica, sans-
serif;")
$txtstream->WriteLine("   }")
$txtstream->WriteLine("   table")
$txtstream->WriteLine("   }")
$txtstream->WriteLine("      BORDER-RIGHT: #999999 3px solid;")
$txtstream->WriteLine("      PADDING-RIGHT: 6px;")
$txtstream->WriteLine("      PADDING-LEFT: 6px;")
$txtstream->WriteLine("      FONT-WEIGHT: Bold;")
$txtstream->WriteLine("      FONT-SIZE: 14px;")
$txtstream->WriteLine("      PADDING-BOTTOM: 6px;")
$txtstream->WriteLine("      COLOR: Peru;")
$txtstream->WriteLine("      LINE-HEIGHT: 14px;")
$txtstream->WriteLine("      PADDING-TOP: 6px;")
$txtstream->WriteLine("      BORDER-BOTTOM: #999 1px solid;")
```

```
$txtstream->WriteLine("        BACKGROUND-COLOR: #eeeeee;")
$txtstream->WriteLine("          FONT-FAMILY: verdana, arial, helvetica, sans-serif;")
$txtstream->WriteLine("        FONT-SIZE: 12px;")
$txtstream->WriteLine("    }")
$txtstream->WriteLine("    th")
$txtstream->WriteLine("    }")
$txtstream->WriteLine("        BORDER-RIGHT: #999999 3px solid;")
$txtstream->WriteLine("        PADDING-RIGHT: 6px;")
$txtstream->WriteLine("        PADDING-LEFT: 6px;")
$txtstream->WriteLine("        FONT-WEIGHT: Bold;")
$txtstream->WriteLine("        FONT-SIZE: 14px;")
$txtstream->WriteLine("        PADDING-BOTTOM: 6px;")
$txtstream->WriteLine("        COLOR: darkred;")
$txtstream->WriteLine("        LINE-HEIGHT: 14px;")
$txtstream->WriteLine("        PADDING-TOP: 6px;")
$txtstream->WriteLine("        BORDER-BOTTOM: #999 1px solid;")
$txtstream->WriteLine("        BACKGROUND-COLOR: #eeeeee;")
$txtstream->WriteLine("        FONT-FAMILY:font-family: Cambria, serif;")
$txtstream->WriteLine("        FONT-SIZE: 12px;")
$txtstream->WriteLine("        text-align: left;")
$txtstream->WriteLine("        white-Space: nowrap;")
$txtstream->WriteLine("    }")
$txtstream->WriteLine("    .th")
$txtstream->WriteLine("    }")
$txtstream->WriteLine("        BORDER-RIGHT: #999999 2px solid;")
$txtstream->WriteLine("        PADDING-RIGHT: 6px;")
$txtstream->WriteLine("        PADDING-LEFT: 6px;")
$txtstream->WriteLine("        FONT-WEIGHT: Bold;")
$txtstream->WriteLine("        PADDING-BOTTOM: 6px;")
$txtstream->WriteLine("        COLOR: black;")
$txtstream->WriteLine("        PADDING-TOP: 6px;")
$txtstream->WriteLine("        BORDER-BOTTOM: #999 2px solid;")
```

```
$txtstream->WriteLine("        BACKGROUND-COLOR: #eeeeee;")
$txtstream->WriteLine("        FONT-FAMILY: font-family: Cambria, serif;")
$txtstream->WriteLine("        FONT-SIZE: 10px;")
$txtstream->WriteLine("        text-align: right;")
$txtstream->WriteLine("        white-Space: nowrap;")
$txtstream->WriteLine("    }")
$txtstream->WriteLine("    td")
$txtstream->WriteLine("    }")
$txtstream->WriteLine("        BORDER-RIGHT: #999999 3px solid;")
$txtstream->WriteLine("        PADDING-RIGHT: 6px;")
$txtstream->WriteLine("        PADDING-LEFT: 6px;")
$txtstream->WriteLine("        FONT-WEIGHT: Normal;")
$txtstream->WriteLine("        PADDING-BOTTOM: 6px;")
$txtstream->WriteLine("        COLOR: navy;")
$txtstream->WriteLine("        LINE-HEIGHT: 14px;")
$txtstream->WriteLine("        PADDING-TOP: 6px;")
$txtstream->WriteLine("        BORDER-BOTTOM: #999 1px solid;")
$txtstream->WriteLine("        BACKGROUND-COLOR: #eeeeee;")
$txtstream->WriteLine("        FONT-FAMILY: font-family: Cambria, serif;")
$txtstream->WriteLine("        FONT-SIZE: 12px;")
$txtstream->WriteLine("        text-align: left;")
$txtstream->WriteLine("        white-Space: nowrap;")
$txtstream->WriteLine("    }")
$txtstream->WriteLine("    div")
$txtstream->WriteLine("    }")
$txtstream->WriteLine("        BORDER-RIGHT: #999999 3px solid;")
$txtstream->WriteLine("        PADDING-RIGHT: 6px;")
$txtstream->WriteLine("        PADDING-LEFT: 6px;")
$txtstream->WriteLine("        FONT-WEIGHT: Normal;")
$txtstream->WriteLine("        PADDING-BOTTOM: 6px;")
$txtstream->WriteLine("        COLOR: white;")
$txtstream->WriteLine("        PADDING-TOP: 6px;")
$txtstream->WriteLine("        BORDER-BOTTOM: #999 1px solid;")
```

```
$txtstream->WriteLine("    BACKGROUND-COLOR: navy;")
$txtstream->WriteLine("    FONT-FAMILY: font-family: Cambria, serif;")
$txtstream->WriteLine("    FONT-SIZE: 10px;")
$txtstream->WriteLine("    text-align: left;")
$txtstream->WriteLine("    white-Space: nowrap;")
$txtstream->WriteLine("  }")
$txtstream->WriteLine("  span")
$txtstream->WriteLine("  }")
$txtstream->WriteLine("    BORDER-RIGHT: #999999 3px solid;")
$txtstream->WriteLine("    PADDING-RIGHT: 3px;")
$txtstream->WriteLine("    PADDING-LEFT: 3px;")
$txtstream->WriteLine("    FONT-WEIGHT: Normal;")
$txtstream->WriteLine("    PADDING-BOTTOM: 3px;")
$txtstream->WriteLine("    COLOR: white;")
$txtstream->WriteLine("    PADDING-TOP: 3px;")
$txtstream->WriteLine("    BORDER-BOTTOM: #999 1px solid;")
$txtstream->WriteLine("    BACKGROUND-COLOR: navy;")
$txtstream->WriteLine("    FONT-FAMILY: font-family: Cambria, serif;")
$txtstream->WriteLine("    FONT-SIZE: 10px;")
$txtstream->WriteLine("    text-align: left;")
$txtstream->WriteLine("    white-Space: nowrap;")
$txtstream->WriteLine("    display:inline-block;")
$txtstream->WriteLine("    width: 100%;")
$txtstream->WriteLine("  }")
$txtstream->WriteLine("  textarea")
$txtstream->WriteLine("  }")
$txtstream->WriteLine("    BORDER-RIGHT: #999999 3px solid;")
$txtstream->WriteLine("    PADDING-RIGHT: 3px;")
$txtstream->WriteLine("    PADDING-LEFT: 3px;")
$txtstream->WriteLine("    FONT-WEIGHT: Normal;")
$txtstream->WriteLine("    PADDING-BOTTOM: 3px;")
$txtstream->WriteLine("    COLOR: white;")
$txtstream->WriteLine("    PADDING-TOP: 3px;")
```

```
$txtstream->WriteLine("          BORDER-BOTTOM: #999 1px solid;")
$txtstream->WriteLine("          BACKGROUND-COLOR: navy;")
$txtstream->WriteLine("          FONT-FAMILY: font-family: Cambria, serif;")
$txtstream->WriteLine("          FONT-SIZE: 10px;")
$txtstream->WriteLine("          text-align: left;")
$txtstream->WriteLine("          white-Space: nowrap;")
$txtstream->WriteLine("          width: 100%;")
$txtstream->WriteLine("     }")
$txtstream->WriteLine("     select")
$txtstream->WriteLine("     }")
$txtstream->WriteLine("          BORDER-RIGHT: #999999 3px solid;")
$txtstream->WriteLine("          PADDING-RIGHT: 6px;")
$txtstream->WriteLine("          PADDING-LEFT: 6px;")
$txtstream->WriteLine("          FONT-WEIGHT: Normal;")
$txtstream->WriteLine("          PADDING-BOTTOM: 6px;")
$txtstream->WriteLine("          COLOR: white;")
$txtstream->WriteLine("          PADDING-TOP: 6px;")
$txtstream->WriteLine("          BORDER-BOTTOM: #999 1px solid;")
$txtstream->WriteLine("          BACKGROUND-COLOR: navy;")
$txtstream->WriteLine("          FONT-FAMILY: font-family: Cambria, serif;")
$txtstream->WriteLine("          FONT-SIZE: 10px;")
$txtstream->WriteLine("          text-align: left;")
$txtstream->WriteLine("          white-Space: nowrap;")
$txtstream->WriteLine("          width: 100%;")
$txtstream->WriteLine("     }")
$txtstream->WriteLine("     input")
$txtstream->WriteLine("     }")
$txtstream->WriteLine("          BORDER-RIGHT: #999999 3px solid;")
$txtstream->WriteLine("          PADDING-RIGHT: 3px;")
$txtstream->WriteLine("          PADDING-LEFT: 3px;")
$txtstream->WriteLine("          FONT-WEIGHT: Bold;")
$txtstream->WriteLine("          PADDING-BOTTOM: 3px;")
$txtstream->WriteLine("          COLOR: white;")
```

```
$txtstream->WriteLine("        PADDING-TOP: 3px;")
$txtstream->WriteLine("        BORDER-BOTTOM: #999 1px solid;")
$txtstream->WriteLine("        BACKGROUND-COLOR: navy;")
$txtstream->WriteLine("        FONT-FAMILY: font-family: Cambria, serif;")
$txtstream->WriteLine("        FONT-SIZE: 12px;")
$txtstream->WriteLine("        text-align: left;")
$txtstream->WriteLine("        display:table-cell;")
$txtstream->WriteLine("        white-Space: nowrap;")
$txtstream->WriteLine("        width: 100%;")
$txtstream->WriteLine("    }")
$txtstream->WriteLine("    h1 }")
$txtstream->WriteLine("    color: antiquewhite;")
$txtstream->WriteLine("    text-shadow: 1px 1px 1px black;")
$txtstream->WriteLine("    padding: 3px;")
$txtstream->WriteLine("    text-align: center;")
$txtstream->WriteLine("      box-shadow: inset 2px 2px 5px rgba(0,0,0,0.5);, inset -2px -2px 5px rgba(255,255,255,0.5);;")
$txtstream->WriteLine("    }")
$txtstream->WriteLine("    </style>');
```

SHADOW BOX

```
$txtstream->WriteLine("    <style type='text/css'>');
$txtstream->WriteLine("    body")
$txtstream->WriteLine("    }")
$txtstream->WriteLine("      PADDING-RIGHT: 0px;")
$txtstream->WriteLine("      PADDING-LEFT: 0px;")
$txtstream->WriteLine("      PADDING-BOTTOM: 0px;")
$txtstream->WriteLine("      MARGIN: 0px;")
$txtstream->WriteLine("      COLOR: #333;")
$txtstream->WriteLine("      PADDING-TOP: 0px;")
$txtstream->WriteLine("        FONT-FAMILY: verdana, arial, helvetica, sans-serif;")
```

```
$txtstream->WriteLine("    }")
$txtstream->WriteLine("    table")
$txtstream->WriteLine("    }")
$txtstream->WriteLine("        BORDER-RIGHT: #999999 1px solid;")
$txtstream->WriteLine("        PADDING-RIGHT: 1px;")
$txtstream->WriteLine("        PADDING-LEFT: 1px;")
$txtstream->WriteLine("        PADDING-BOTTOM: 1px;")
$txtstream->WriteLine("        LINE-HEIGHT: 8px;")
$txtstream->WriteLine("        PADDING-TOP: 1px;")
$txtstream->WriteLine("        BORDER-BOTTOM: #999 1px solid;")
$txtstream->WriteLine("        BACKGROUND-COLOR: #eeeeee;")
$txtstream->WriteLine("
filter:progid:DXImageTransform.Microsoft.Shadow(color='silver',        Direction=135,
Strength=16")
$txtstream->WriteLine("    }")
$txtstream->WriteLine("    th")
$txtstream->WriteLine("    }")
$txtstream->WriteLine("        BORDER-RIGHT: #999999 3px solid;")
$txtstream->WriteLine("        PADDING-RIGHT: 6px;")
$txtstream->WriteLine("        PADDING-LEFT: 6px;")
$txtstream->WriteLine("        FONT-WEIGHT: Bold;")
$txtstream->WriteLine("        FONT-SIZE: 14px;")
$txtstream->WriteLine("        PADDING-BOTTOM: 6px;")
$txtstream->WriteLine("        COLOR: darkred;")
$txtstream->WriteLine("        LINE-HEIGHT: 14px;")
$txtstream->WriteLine("        PADDING-TOP: 6px;")
$txtstream->WriteLine("        BORDER-BOTTOM: #999 1px solid;")
$txtstream->WriteLine("        BACKGROUND-COLOR: #eeeeee;")
$txtstream->WriteLine("        FONT-FAMILY: font-family: Cambria, serif;")
$txtstream->WriteLine("        FONT-SIZE: 12px;")
$txtstream->WriteLine("        text-align: left;")
$txtstream->WriteLine("        white-Space: nowrap;")
$txtstream->WriteLine("    }")
```

```
$txtstream->WriteLine(“    .th”)
$txtstream->WriteLine(“    }”)
$txtstream->WriteLine(“        BORDER-RIGHT: #999999 2px solid;”)
$txtstream->WriteLine(“        PADDING-RIGHT: 6px;”)
$txtstream->WriteLine(“        PADDING-LEFT: 6px;”)
$txtstream->WriteLine(“        FONT-WEIGHT: Bold;”)
$txtstream->WriteLine(“        PADDING-BOTTOM: 6px;”)
$txtstream->WriteLine(“        COLOR: black;”)
$txtstream->WriteLine(“        PADDING-TOP: 6px;”)
$txtstream->WriteLine(“        BORDER-BOTTOM: #999 2px solid;”)
$txtstream->WriteLine(“        BACKGROUND-COLOR: #eeeeee;”)
$txtstream->WriteLine(“        FONT-FAMILY: font-family: Cambria, serif;”)
$txtstream->WriteLine(“        FONT-SIZE: 10px;”)
$txtstream->WriteLine(“        text-align: right;”)
$txtstream->WriteLine(“        white-Space: nowrap;”)
$txtstream->WriteLine(“    }”)
$txtstream->WriteLine(“    td”)
$txtstream->WriteLine(“    }”)
$txtstream->WriteLine(“        BORDER-RIGHT: #999999 3px solid;”)
$txtstream->WriteLine(“        PADDING-RIGHT: 6px;”)
$txtstream->WriteLine(“        PADDING-LEFT: 6px;”)
$txtstream->WriteLine(“        FONT-WEIGHT: Normal;”)
$txtstream->WriteLine(“        PADDING-BOTTOM: 6px;”)
$txtstream->WriteLine(“        COLOR: navy;”)
$txtstream->WriteLine(“        LINE-HEIGHT: 14px;”)
$txtstream->WriteLine(“        PADDING-TOP: 6px;”)
$txtstream->WriteLine(“        BORDER-BOTTOM: #999 1px solid;”)
$txtstream->WriteLine(“        BACKGROUND-COLOR: #eeeeee;”)
$txtstream->WriteLine(“        FONT-FAMILY: font-family: Cambria, serif;”)
$txtstream->WriteLine(“        FONT-SIZE: 12px;”)
$txtstream->WriteLine(“        text-align: left;”)
$txtstream->WriteLine(“        white-Space: nowrap;”)
$txtstream->WriteLine(“    }”)
```

```
$txtstream->WriteLine("    div")
$txtstream->WriteLine("    }")
$txtstream->WriteLine("        BORDER-RIGHT: #999999 3px solid;")
$txtstream->WriteLine("        PADDING-RIGHT: 6px;")
$txtstream->WriteLine("        PADDING-LEFT: 6px;")
$txtstream->WriteLine("        FONT-WEIGHT: Normal;")
$txtstream->WriteLine("        PADDING-BOTTOM: 6px;")
$txtstream->WriteLine("        COLOR: white;")
$txtstream->WriteLine("        PADDING-TOP: 6px;")
$txtstream->WriteLine("        BORDER-BOTTOM: #999 1px solid;")
$txtstream->WriteLine("        BACKGROUND-COLOR: navy;")
$txtstream->WriteLine("        FONT-FAMILY: font-family: Cambria, serif;")
$txtstream->WriteLine("        FONT-SIZE: 10px;")
$txtstream->WriteLine("        text-align: left;")
$txtstream->WriteLine("        white-Space: nowrap;")
$txtstream->WriteLine("    }")
$txtstream->WriteLine("    span")
$txtstream->WriteLine("    }")
$txtstream->WriteLine("        BORDER-RIGHT: #999999 3px solid;")
$txtstream->WriteLine("        PADDING-RIGHT: 3px;")
$txtstream->WriteLine("        PADDING-LEFT: 3px;")
$txtstream->WriteLine("        FONT-WEIGHT: Normal;")
$txtstream->WriteLine("        PADDING-BOTTOM: 3px;")
$txtstream->WriteLine("        COLOR: white;")
$txtstream->WriteLine("        PADDING-TOP: 3px;")
$txtstream->WriteLine("        BORDER-BOTTOM: #999 1px solid;")
$txtstream->WriteLine("        BACKGROUND-COLOR: navy;")
$txtstream->WriteLine("        FONT-FAMILY: font-family: Cambria, serif;")
$txtstream->WriteLine("        FONT-SIZE: 10px;")
$txtstream->WriteLine("        text-align: left;")
$txtstream->WriteLine("        white-Space: nowrap;")
$txtstream->WriteLine("        display: inline-block;")
$txtstream->WriteLine("        width: 100%;")
```

```
$txtstream->WriteLine("    }")
$txtstream->WriteLine("   textarea")
$txtstream->WriteLine("    }")
$txtstream->WriteLine("        BORDER-RIGHT: #999999 3px solid;")
$txtstream->WriteLine("        PADDING-RIGHT: 3px;")
$txtstream->WriteLine("        PADDING-LEFT: 3px;")
$txtstream->WriteLine("        FONT-WEIGHT: Normal;")
$txtstream->WriteLine("        PADDING-BOTTOM: 3px;")
$txtstream->WriteLine("        COLOR: white;")
$txtstream->WriteLine("        PADDING-TOP: 3px;")
$txtstream->WriteLine("        BORDER-BOTTOM: #999 1px solid;")
$txtstream->WriteLine("        BACKGROUND-COLOR: navy;")
$txtstream->WriteLine("        FONT-FAMILY: font-family: Cambria, serif;")
$txtstream->WriteLine("        FONT-SIZE: 10px;")
$txtstream->WriteLine("        text-align: left;")
$txtstream->WriteLine("        white-Space: nowrap;")
$txtstream->WriteLine("        width: 100%;")
$txtstream->WriteLine("    }")
$txtstream->WriteLine("   select")
$txtstream->WriteLine("    }")
$txtstream->WriteLine("        BORDER-RIGHT: #999999 3px solid;")
$txtstream->WriteLine("        PADDING-RIGHT: 6px;")
$txtstream->WriteLine("        PADDING-LEFT: 6px;")
$txtstream->WriteLine("        FONT-WEIGHT: Normal;")
$txtstream->WriteLine("        PADDING-BOTTOM: 6px;")
$txtstream->WriteLine("        COLOR: white;")
$txtstream->WriteLine("        PADDING-TOP: 6px;")
$txtstream->WriteLine("        BORDER-BOTTOM: #999 1px solid;")
$txtstream->WriteLine("        BACKGROUND-COLOR: navy;")
$txtstream->WriteLine("        FONT-FAMILY: font-family: Cambria, serif;")
$txtstream->WriteLine("        FONT-SIZE: 10px;")
$txtstream->WriteLine("        text-align: left;")
$txtstream->WriteLine("        white-Space: nowrap;")
```

```
$txtstream->WriteLine("     width: 100%;")
$txtstream->WriteLine("   }")
$txtstream->WriteLine("   input")
$txtstream->WriteLine("   }")
$txtstream->WriteLine("     BORDER-RIGHT: #999999 3px solid;")
$txtstream->WriteLine("     PADDING-RIGHT: 3px;")
$txtstream->WriteLine("     PADDING-LEFT: 3px;")
$txtstream->WriteLine("     FONT-WEIGHT: Bold;")
$txtstream->WriteLine("     PADDING-BOTTOM: 3px;")
$txtstream->WriteLine("     COLOR: white;")
$txtstream->WriteLine("     PADDING-TOP: 3px;")
$txtstream->WriteLine("     BORDER-BOTTOM: #999 1px solid;")
$txtstream->WriteLine("     BACKGROUND-COLOR: navy;")
$txtstream->WriteLine("     FONT-FAMILY: font-family: Cambria, serif;")
$txtstream->WriteLine("     FONT-SIZE: 12px;")
$txtstream->WriteLine("     text-align: left;")
$txtstream->WriteLine("     display: table-cell;")
$txtstream->WriteLine("     white-Space: nowrap;")
$txtstream->WriteLine("     width: 100%;")
$txtstream->WriteLine("   }")
$txtstream->WriteLine("   h1 }")
$txtstream->WriteLine("   color: antiquewhite;")
$txtstream->WriteLine("   text-shadow: 1px 1px 1px black;")
$txtstream->WriteLine("   padding: 3px;")
$txtstream->WriteLine("   text-align: center;")
$txtstream->WriteLine("     box-shadow: inset 2px 2px 5px rgba(0,0,0,0.5);,
inset -2px -2px 5px rgba(255,255,255,0.5);;")
$txtstream->WriteLine("   }")
$txtstream->WriteLine("   </style>');
```

www.ingramcontent.com/pod-product-compliance
Lightning Source LLC
Chambersburg PA
CBHW071549080326
40690CB00056B/1610